Pink Shoes and Jilbaab

Not Your Average Hijab Guide

Kiran Shah

Pink Shoes and Jilbaab
Copyright © 2021 Kiran Shah
First published in 2021

Print: 978-1-922456-24-3
E-book: 978-1-922456-25-0
Hardback: 978-1-922456-28-1

All rights reserved. No part of this book may be reproduced, stored in a retrieval system, or transmitted by any means (electronic, mechanical, photocopying, recording, or otherwise) without written permission from the author.

Because of the dynamic nature of the Internet, any web addresses or links contained in this book may have changed since publication and may no longer be valid. The information in this book is based on the author's experiences and opinions. The views expressed in this book are solely those of the author and do not necessarily reflect the views of the publisher; the publisher hereby disclaims any responsibility for them.

The author of this book does not dispense any form of medical, legal, financial, or technical advice either directly or indirectly. The intent of the author is solely to provide information of a general nature to help you in your quest for personal development and growth. In the event you use any of the information in this book, the author and the publisher assume no responsibility for your actions. If any form of expert assistance is required, the services of a competent professional should be sought.

Publishing information
Publishing, design, and production facilitated by Passionpreneur Publishing,
A division of Passionpreneur Organization Pty Ltd
ABN: 48640637529

www.PassionpreneurPublishing.com
Melbourne, VIC | Australia

TESTIMONIALS

I have three words to express how this book made me feel: "This is me," OR "I can relate."

I know what you're thinking, another feely book—spoiler alert! It's not.

Every Muslim woman alive can resonate with every word in it; it reflects grace and resilience with a fierce motivation that makes one go, "I can do this!" I have read many books on coaching and self-belief, but this book speaks to me at both personal and professional levels. The journey of self-discovery, based on reliance on Allah, empathy, and the power of forgiveness, is a true reflection of every thought expressed. The author's words and what she is trying to communicate linger for long after you finish the book—we are all more than what we say and much more than what we don't.

— **Shadab Kazi**
Founder, The Crateful Mom

One of the great gifts that Kiran has are her unique observation skills—taking it all in, making small mental notes of all the complexities around, and then pouring her thoughts out like water, smooth and subtle. Her words are strong and find their way through difficult and complicated topics, leaving a trail that imprints itself on the mind of the reader.

Her attention to detail while penning down her stream of thoughts makes the process of reading her work a pleasurable exercise!

I am sure you will enjoy reading this book.

— **Swaleha Atif**
Banking professional

Kiran has brought in a unique twist to the challenging topic of balancing *hijab* values with being hip and cool.

— **Moustafa Hamwi**
Passionpreneur Publishing

Kiran is a rare find in today's world. Her soul is beautiful, and she expresses this through creative mediums such as her art and writing. She is authentic and does not believe in sugarcoating her points of view; her emotions run deep and her insights and reflections on moments and people run even deeper. Her wit is dry as is her unique sense of humor, and I love that about her!

— **Maissa Al Khafajy**
Senior Communications professional

"It was refreshing to read a book that is relatable in so many ways and touches your soul—I imagined myself as a teenager and relived every emotion that I had felt when I began my *hijab* journey. If only the book had been written and I had had the opportunity to read it when I was 16. You were right Kiran, Pink Shoes and Jilbaab talks to you like a friend!

The book is loaded with motivation, reflections, emotion, and what not. Just what young girls need. A must-read!

— **Sheza Qamar**
Play Therapist, Dyslexia Teacher, Motivational Speaker &
Podcaster

"Kiran puts all her knowledge amidst the pages, in black and white. She wholeheartedly offers all the wisdom she has gained through her experiences and the maturity that it has brought on to help young girls along on their journey with faith, grace, and conviction and above all, with a true understanding of religious values."

— **Hoda Elsobky**
Happiness Mentor and author of Dare to be Happy

Sister Kiran has been my mentor and guide for a number of years, and her wise words have helped me understand the *hijab*. Her intellect and teaching abilities are matched by her kindness and ability to connect with her students and readers.

— **Dr. Sumbal Riaz**

I had a session with Kiran and was very happy with the result. She discussed my fears and apprehensions, and my goals in life and seamlessly helped me put them together in a way that I could no longer feel or see the reasons for the fears and doubts that I started with. Kiran has always been a very genuine person who one can easily relate with. She speaks very frankly of her own points of view, making it easy to open up to her.

— **Najma Salman**
Director-Client Manager, MEA for an international bank

Throughout my life, I have had an off and on relationship with my *hijab*. It was during those downtimes when my ego and the world got in the way of my *hijab* that I needed a hand to pull me back up the ladder. That hand was Kiran's. No one tried harder than her to make sure that my slips weren't too far down.

Through her persistence, without being badgering, her hopeful words, her quiet acceptance when she felt it was needed, and her lifestyle as an example, she has helped me on my journey, and I know that she will always be there.

Kiran has helped my journey with hijab, through the

ups and downs, with friendship, hope, acceptance, wisdom, and kind grace.

— **Reja Shahzad**
Housewife, UK

Kiran is a beautiful soul that is on this earth to love, to teach by example, and to demonstrate how life can be amazing. Her vision and her creativity are so aligned with her heart that she can't help but create beauty on canvas, on paper, and in people. She loves life and she loves people. In everything she does, she sprinkles that sparkle and glitter that is her aligned and powerful influence. God blessed her with beauty, a loving heart, creative vision, powerful speaking and writing skills, and amazing compassionate people around. She is a kind, gentle, and creative soul who is on a journey of creating great things, an exhilarating experience to watch.

— **Dana Sunnatulla**
Meditation expert

I love Kiran's way of dealing with emotional issues. With her, I felt understood, taken care of, and softly handled, while getting to the root of my issue. She helped me a lot with my phobia as well. Professionalism and softness best describe her style of therapy. I definitely recommend her. ☆☆☆☆☆

— **Vivien Helacs**
Hypnotherapist and NLP coach

Kiran is a truthful lady. She is committed to bridging the gaps in your inner self, bringing your hidden potentials out, and developing them to their fullest in achieving the very best of yourself. An empathetic and forward-looking coach.

— **Dashyni Laporte**
NLP practitioner

Kiran is very easy to communicate with. She's a patient and sensitive listener. Along with these two qualities, she always has that spark of excitement for new projects. I have commissioned her for one of my dream projects, and she is making it come true in gradual steps. She's working on a very large scale "Stamp Series" for me and is as committed to its completion as I am. I'm glad that this journey has taken off with a talented artist like Kiran, whose dedication will make it an experience that my family will cherish for generations to come.

— **Wajiha Azeem**
Founder, Seashells and Pearls

I had the pleasure of working with Kiran. She is an absolute inspiration for women. Her passion to help young girls and women in Pakistan is truly inspirational. Her dedication and commitment towards her book and running the marathon is a reminder to women that power lies within them.

— **Ankita Magdani**
Clinical hypnotherapist/psychotherapist

I've rarely come across professionals that have sheer talent and relevant concepts combined with an impeccable work ethic. Kiran is self-motivated, highly articulate in her work, and able to lead a project from conceptualisation to final delivery. Highly recommended!

— **Khurram Alvi**
Writer/Director, Animated feature films and series

Working with Kiran Shah was an absolute pleasure. She was always punctual and focused on the task at hand with utmost dedication. Kiran is very dedicated and yearns to learn new things. She has this phenomenal enthusiasm that is incredibly contagious. Her vibrant presence in group projects keeps the ambience at work engaging and radiant. She will be a valuable asset to any team.

— **Amber Kazmi**
Visual artist

This book is dedicated to my dear husband.

Thank you for letting me be the best version of myself.

(I owe you a chapter Mr. Pink Shoes and Jilbaab. Maybe in the next book 😉)

CONTENTS

Acknowledgements	13
Introduction	15
Do It Like You Mean It!	
Chapter 1	19
Painted Nails and the Other Dimension	
Chapter 2	27
The Game-Changer	
Chapter 3	35
The Ultimate Connection	
Chapter 4	47
Strengthening the Core	
Chapter 5	63
I Look Horrible	
Chapter 6	73
The Grit	
Chapter 7	85
Burj Khalifa of Dreams	
Chapter 8	99
Be a Mouthful	
Chapter 9	111
Grace	

Chapter 10 123
Why Did She Take It Off?

Chapter 11 137
But What About Love?

Conclusion 147
There Is No Tomorrow

Glossary 153

About the Author 159

ACKNOWLEDGEMENTS

I would like to thank my mum, for being the most courageous person I know. I see a reflection of you in me, Mama, and I am following the same path of philanthropy as you.

I would like to thank my Abu for giving me the best memories of my childhood which stay within me no matter what. Those memories have come up repeatedly in my book.

I would like to thank my children, Mikaeel, Hayaa, Hoorain, and Musab. You are the light of my life; not a day goes by without me thanking Allah for the blessings that he has bestowed upon me through you. A special thanks to the older ones for their continuous support and advice; and for reading my chapters and telling me that it would work!

I would like to thank my siblings, Tashna Salim, Talha Salim, and Mustafa Salim, for always being there for me.

I would like to offer the biggest thanks to all the young girls who came forward to help me with my project. It was not possible to write a book without knowing the issues or questions that go on in their minds. Thank you, Zayyena Shoaib Anwar, Heba Shoaib Anwar, Fatima Baber, Wania Ehsan, Maisha Ehsan, Zoya Adeel, Pareysa Ahmed, Maira Ahmed, Zaina Ahmed, Rehab Khan, Waniya Jaffri, Safa Mohammed Umer, Fizza Muhib, Muzna Qamar, and Aaminah Adnan (and all her friends). I hope I was able to answer all your questions.

I would especially like to thank my girl gang for the continuous support and ideas. I don't want to mention names for the fear of missing out any. I am blessed to be surrounded by amazing women who know how to support each other.

Thanks are in order for my book club buddies who came to my rescue and answered all my weird queries! You guys rock!

Special thanks to Zayyena Shoaib Anwar for the feedback. You hold a special place in my heart. May you always achieve everything you aim for!

Heartfelt gratitude to Farin Zaman and Fariaa Israr for their ideas. I would like to dedicate Chapter 10 to Fariaa for highlighting the importance of this topic and for all her help with collecting the data.

I am grateful to Sharmeen Ehsan for her continuous support. I would like to dedicate Chapter 11 to you, my dear friend, for the ideas. I have tried to pour it into the chapter to the best of my ability.

Sheza Qamar, I am indebted to you for your continued support and more! You mean the world to me. Love you to the moon and back!

Another special thanks to Thanaya Asghar for your continuous support. It is surprising to know that people whom we have never met can become the best source of support and inspiration. I owe you so much!

I would also like to thank Humaira Nasim for inviting me to her book launch and reuniting me with Passionpreneur Publishing once again. This book would not have come to life if it wasn't for you. Hope you see and recognise some insights from our discussions in the book.

Finally, I would like to thank Moustafa Hamwi and the team at Passionpreneur Publishing for all their hard work and commitment. This book couldn't happen without you all.

INTRODUCTION

Do It Like You Mean It!

"Be a Girl with a Mind,
a Woman with Attitude,
and a Lady with Class."

— Anonymous

My dear girls,
Life is a roller coaster, and you are required to make a whole lot of decisions while you are on it. Sounds tough? Oh yes, it is!

Tell me something honestly, has it been hard to balance your *Deen* and *Dunya*?

Like a see-saw, maybe! One side too heavy, or the other.

Too *deeni* for the *dunya* clan and too *dunya* for the *deeni* clan?

Tell you what, it is the same for me too!

The journey of balancing the two worlds is tough; let me give that to you. But we can't really hide from it, can we? The best we can do is to give it the best we've got!

If I tell you that I have answers to all your questions, I'd be lying. What I do have is a basket full of dorky experiences that might give you an insight into what is truly important.

It is very brave of you to pick up a book off a shelf that looks nothing like a religious book should. But really, is there anything perfect in this world?

If you haven't put the book back on the shelf and run a mile away, let me tell you that this book—as the name suggests—is a cocktail of my experiences, religious, and others. In my hike to get on top of being the best version of myself, I have picked up a few things that might just help you too! But hey, no pressure.

I don't believe in pressure. I don't believe in force. Instead, I believe in humour, and I feel it does the job quite well. I have always learnt the best from the teachers who are able to crack a few jokes here and there. It makes them more relatable, and more human.

In reality, I am one of those socially awkward people who say Happy Birthday to the waiter instead of thank you—one of those people who is always wearing a tight smile, wondering where my hands should go, always under the pressure of trying to say the right thing, and always doing the opposite. A better writer than a socialite any day. Hence, this book.

So yes, this is my first introduction to you—the socially awkward Ms. Kiran Shah. Mum of four. Teacher to many, and a friend to a whole lot of them. An artist, a writer, a Life Coach, a fitness enthusiast, and a foodie.

My journey is a pure comical one. I took up the *hijab* and left it. Took it up again, and left it again. The third time it stuck with me—for over a decade now. You could say the first two were failed attempts. I would say they were learning experiences—po-ta-to, po-tah-to—same thing. The glass is almost always full for me, unless I break it. And if I do, I sit by it for a while and then go looking for another one.

What would you get from this book you'd ask?

The glass half-full, I'd say. Lesson number one of this Book. I am as imperfect as imperfect can be, but I never give up. And that's the essence of everything in life, isn't it? In *Deen* and in *Dunya*, never to give up. And that's what I'll make you do. Never give up! Get up, and get things done!

Number two of the most important lessons, to **never lose yourself in the pursuit of perfection**. Be you. There is only one You Allah has created, and there is a purpose for it. Find that purpose, find God, and find you.

Number three: **know your stuff, girl!** You can't be what you know nothing about. Since this book is about *hijab*, it will educate you about what *hijab* is, as per the Book of Allah, and give you tips on how to make it work in today's competitive world.

Number four: **how to be a dream catcher!** Not one of those dingly-dangly things but the real deal. Dreams are what keep life interesting. That rush, that adrenaline. And if we don't have that, what's the point of it all?

Number five: There is no number five!

Go read the book!

Much love,
Kiran Shah

1

PAINTED NAILS AND THE OTHER DIMENSION

> Don't be afraid to take a big step. You can't
> cross a chasm in two small jumps.
>
> — David Lloyd George

I remember walking down the streets of Dubai in a white T-shirt and jeans—some twelve years ago. Also the warm October breeze on my face; feeling so damn good. And why wouldn't I be? I was young, twenty-five to be exact; married to the person I loved; and recently moved to the UAE. Two kids, me and him—it was the perfect proportion. We had the cutest two-bed apartment, which I absolutely loved and was in the process of decorating. I would dance-walk my way through the day and so would the ideas in my head. Everything was just perfect. I could finally have the life I always wanted. Woopie dee doo!

I come from Pakistan, you see, the land of close family ties and a superb amount of interference. So, to be away from that place was my chance to make a life of my own. Did I have any idea of what that was? No, not really. But I was going to have a great life and make my own rules.

I was going to have the *halwa* and eat it too!

But did I know I'll be a *hijabi* within a few months of moving to such a modern city? No ma'am, not in my wildest dreams. As a gesture of thanks to God for giving me the life I had always wanted, I wanted to learn a bit about my religion. Nothing major, just the basics. You see, I am a curious person. I like to know and experience things on my own. In most cases, it has landed me into quite some interesting scenarios, and like most times, I had no idea where this particular curiosity would lead me.

Funnily enough, religion had been a guarded territory for us Pakistanis all our lives. I can't speak for all, but generally, it's like, "Be enough of a Muslim that you do (generic) good, but nothing over the top." ("Don't go all *Mullah*!" is the general expectation.) And so, I was decent enough to want to know what the Quran says, but impetuous enough to not resist an invite to a dance party (which, for the record and my utter disappointment, I did not receive in Dubai. Imagine… IN DUBAI! IN THE LAND OF GLORIOUS NIGHTLIFE! Not even one invite!).

And so, back to me in my white T-shirt and jeans humming away on the streets of the UAE. There must have been a hint of purity in my intentions when I said I wanted to learn about my *Deen* because, within a few months, I heard of a Quran teacher in my block. I wanted to start immediately, but the issue was, I had nothing decent to wear; all my *shalwar kameezs* had no *shalwars* in them, because capris were in fashion, and all my *kameezs* had no sleeves, because well… I was cool, remember? And so, I landed on her doorstep in jeans and a black top, with a huge shawl trying to hide my sleeveless arms. But she spotted my perfectly manicured hands like a teacher would and said, "You know *wudu* is not valid with the nail colour on, right?" "Yes ma'am," said I, as I stepped into her house and into another dimension.

After almost a year of learning the basics from the teacher in my block (and in this one year transitioning from jeans to *hijab*, and then to *abaya*), I heard of this really cool and organised Quran course being conducted nearby. I went for a trial class and was hooked.

I am a sucker for good literature and chronologically organised information. So for me, this course was a dream come true. I had never imagined religious information to be so interesting and relevant. I was eager and curious, and went in every day with my backpack on, like a little kid. I wanted to know so much more! And before I knew it, I had a diploma in Islamic Studies in my hand. This course was the best thing that had ever happened to me. It was tough, it challenged me, and I spent my day and night studying. I wasn't the best student, but I was most definitely one of the most active.

Fast forward two years and I was teaching in the same institute which had inspired me so much. I started on a very basic job, checking papers and designing bulletin boards, but within a year, I landed on a position I loved. I was one of the Group Leaders and was made Incharge of the new students coming in, in the middle of the course. You know how hard it is to settle in when you enter an institution in the middle of the school year, right? These girls were totally raw, and my job was to fast-track these new admissions and bring them in line with those who were already in the course and were, by this time, much ahead. It was a challenge, and I loved every minute of it. It became a kind of a mission. I had a reason to wake up in the morning (and to run off without doing the dishes). And as amazing as the teaching bit was, I was thrilled to be the Editorial Head as well. I was in charge of writing/designing/proofreading all the literary materials for the institute, which included their brochures, blog, yearly magazine, etc. I was doing what I loved—teaching, writing, editing, and blogging.

The ultimate highlight though was when I was selected

for the school tours. We were basically supposed to go to different schools and give motivational speeches. I remember my first time with an auditorium full of students, approximately a thousand of them. I did a presentation on "The Purpose of Life," which was an absolute hit, and a lot of students gathered around us after the session to ask questions. I can't forget one particular girl who came up to me, grade six I think, almost looking devastated and said, "But how can I serve The Purpose of Life? I love Maths!" like that was the most horrible thing to have happened to her. It was the absolute aww moment for me. We spoke for a bit. I explained to her the importance of a mathematician in a society and how a society would collapse if we had any less of them. How every act of helping others can be counted as worship. By the time I was finished, the smile on her face told me that I had done my job. Inspire one girl and you have inspired a generation. And that, ladies and gentlemen, is exactly what I had done, and I felt marvellous. Did I tell you I am awesome? You'll get to know as you read through.

From there, a series of inspirational courses for the youngsters started. I realised that I had a way with teenagers. Younger than them don't get my looney jokes, so I was stuck with the teens. It went on for a bit. I did many short courses, summer camps, etc. with the teens. I loved my students and my students loved me—the perfect love story. My basic target was to show my students that *Deen* doesn't necessarily have to be boring. YOU have to be creative. Many of them did pick up the beat.

But times change; I had another baby and had to stop working. It was an amazing family time. The house was full and so were my hands, but the creative side of me was going numb from boredom. And so, I started my Facebook blog, Pink Shoes and *Jilbaab*. The time I spent on the blog was my time away from my crazies to spark some of my amazing personas in the form of words (kidding! almost). It was quite sombre, to be honest. I didn't plan on it to be so serious, just that I was very philosophical in those days. Too many children can do that to you. The actual plan was for it to be a chic mom-blog kind of a thing, but that was so much work. Dress up your kids, dress up the house, and have pretty pictures taken of all that we do in a day—of course, it was bound to fail. I was barely keeping them alive, let alone take fancy pictures; hence my blog became kind of like a diary where I would share the lessons from the day, and my modest following would root for me. Job done, I was happy, and so were the followers (or so I hope).

A few years down, and after another kid (by this time there were four, just in case you lost count), I launched Naqsh by Kiran, my artistic venture, which took up very quickly. I had done my Bachelors in Fine Arts some fifteen years back, but I never really got to paint ever since I had kids. In my imagination, kids, paints, smears, handprints, cooking and crying (children and me both) were too much to handle, and hence I had given up/postponed my dream of being an artist, until all of them pack their bags and leave the house. But on continuous bickering from my husband and a lot of encouragement from my friends, I finally got down to painting. I guess my amazing personality wasn't enough to get the money rolling in, and I actually had to move my lazy bum. And so, the artist in me, who had been sleeping for more than a decade, woke up with a jolt. "Are you kidding me?" said he, which I completely ignored and went on painting happily.

The first time my work was exhibited, I thought the gallery had made a mistake. I couldn't have been actually selected. The artist in me was still trying to make sense of it all; I couldn't have become a "real" artist. It hadn't really sunk in. But then a few exhibitions later, *Khaleej Times* included me in their "Women at the Helm" list, and I was like… OKAY! It seemed like we were in business. And before I knew it, I had made it to many exhibitions locally and internationally. And when I had the opportunity to display in the Carrousel du Louvre, I was ecstatic! I immediately made a girls' plan, dumped my kids with my husband, and went to Paris.

As for today, my life is good, Alhamdulillah. Along with all of the above, I am a Master NLP Coach, with the purpose of helping young girls find their way in life. I have achieved everything that I set out to do, and I am very comfortable with myself as a person. This is a journey of twelve years that I have narrated in the shortest way possible. A journey of me in my *hijab*, achieving things that I dreamt of. In these twelve years, there were many stages that I walked through; each had challenges of its own. I learnt a lot. I grew a lot. All by the help of Allah, سُبْحَانَهُ وَتَعَالَىٰ.

Now, why did I tell you my story?

So that you know who this person talking to you is; and so we can build a rapport before I go on yapping about my experiences. How am I supposed to convince you to listen to me if you don't know who I am?

I have been wearing *hijab* for almost twelve years now—twelve years with its share of hiccups (and it was a huge share!). I will be sharing many of them with you throughout the book. I had two failed attempts of wearing *hijab* before the glorious walk in white T-shirt and jeans on the streets of the UAE: once at the age of fourteen, which lasted for a few months, then at the age of eighteen, which went on for almost two years.

The fact that I stopped wearing *hijab* at the time is the biggest proof that I understand the struggle. I understand everyone who is unable to do it or is struggling with the idea. I understand the inner dialogue, anxiety, and fears. I also understand the undeniable urge to please Allah سُبْحَانَهُ وَتَعَالَىٰ despite all of it.

This book is all about trying to balance the fast-moving life and our values. It's all about giving you a heads-up before the hazard even arrives. I know the drill because I was that girl, and I have been around young girls and their issues for more than a decade now. My aim is to help as many girls, like the sixth-grader I met at that school, as possible.

If you have bought this book, chances are you are either on this path already or thinking of joining the club. Let me tell you one thing, and one thing only to start this off with. This is the journey of finding yourself. This is the journey for yourself—not your mom, not your friends, or the Instagrammers that you follow. It is something completely between you and Allah. It is finding your way to Him. Take it on your own terms. *Hijab* may come or may not. I'll try my best, but at the end of the day, it's between you and Him. Every person is different, and everyone has a calling. Find yours to get to your purpose in this life and the other. Take small steps. Have fun and love every moment of it. Yes, you will have doubts; yes, it will be all new and uncomfortable, but don't let go of the good that walks right beside the doubt. Work on it hand in hand. And before you know it, you will own it, and it will own you.

I hope this book serves as the lift that you need right now. To wear the *hijab* (or not), to struggle through life, and to battle all the insecurities that media or the people around you throw at you. You are above the judgements of others, and there is a higher purpose of why you are here in the first place. I hope this book talks to you like your best friend and tells you that we are real, this life is real; and if we are not having a good time following the *Deen* of Allah, there is a malfunction somewhere. Let's try to get it sorted.

> **The first step, my son, which one makes in the world, is the one on which depends the rest of our days.**
>
> — VOLTAIRE

2

THE GAME-CHANGER

> We don't have to waste our time learning how to make pastry when we can use grandma's recipes.
>
> — ORSON DE WITT

Growing up in Pakistan, I don't remember seeing anyone with the proper headgear/*abaya* on. I am sure there must be families who would be adhering to this dress code, but I wasn't exposed to them. In my family, the norm was to wear *dupattas*, as was in most families around us. The *dupatta* may get thinner or completely disappear depending on how cool you think you were. We were a mediocre family. So, a mediocre-sized *dupatta* was good enough for a good girl. Older women would take a shawl only if they are going to a crowded *bazaar*, otherwise, a *dupatta* was good enough for them too. You could have a barely sleeved, lycra fitted *kameezs*, but the *dupatta* would be the proof of your modesty.

The only *burqa* I remember seeing growing up was of the *Imam Sahab*'s wife (now I sound like Kamila Shamsie). We called her *Molvi Sahab*'s wife (as a child, every designation would suffice to be the name of the person, like Carpenter uncle, Tailor Aunty, Bakery-*walay* uncle, etc.). Anyways, *Molvi Sahab*'s wife was the only person I knew who used to wear a *burqa*. I would see people on the streets and markets wearing *burqas*, but I did not know any personally.

Covering the heads was also rare as far as I can remember. It only happened on specific occasions, like if anyone had to pray, when the *azaan* was being called out (though some women would suffice with a cushion or newspaper on the head if the *dupatta* wasn't within their arm's reach), if you were visiting some ultraorthodox bazaar (or relative), or if someone died. The respected *dupatta* would come off instantly when these conditions subsided. Another group of women who covered their heads was the grandma group. In short, growing up, I did not have any interaction with people covering up. The religion practised around me was also of a very cultural value. A high moral criterion was to be followed, but no one really knew why they were doing what they were doing. Everyone knew how to read the Quran fluently, but no one knew the meaning of the words. Everyone knew prayer was *fard*, but they would not necessarily pray five times a day. The Prophet stories were known, but not chronologically. This was the average Pakistani household, and I was a part of it.

My first interaction with the classy Arab-world *abaya* was in 2002. In a well-reputed art institute, where mostly the "burger" kids of Karachi would come, a girl came in with a flowy black *abaya*—front open, a bit of jeans peeping through, and a designer signature on one side of the gown. It looked so elegant and so different that it had my attention right away. Among all the jeans-clad, skimpy shirts, it was that *abaya* that inspired me. I didn't know a *burqa* could actually look stylish. It was modest, it was cool, and it was everything I wanted to be. That girl, Reja Shahzad, then became my best friend, and is very much so till date. Her grandparents lived in Bahrain; no wonder she had access to such lovely modest wear. She was the one who then introduced me to the rise of *Deen* in the elites of Pakistan, which was slowly becoming the "in" thing. It was an absolute revelation for me, to see religion as a proper, organised course of life, not just "a thing" everyone does. She had the education of why she was doing what she was doing, while I was a mere follower of customary Islam. She was informed and enlightened, and so balanced. With her, I tasted the fun in watching *Friends* and eating chips and then getting up to pray, or to have endless discussions on English Literature, art, and then on religion too. With her, I learnt that praying in the car was an actual thing to do when you can't find a place while shopping. She knew the latest fashion trends but was modest too. In her house, I learnt to live Islam. I owe it to her and her family for unknowingly presenting such an example for me that I still follow. They normalised Islam for me; they normalised *hijab* for me. Everything looked do-able; religion didn't seem so secular anymore. It didn't seem like a thing that only *Molvi Sahab*'s wife would do. I could do it too, and I could be a normal, fun-loving teenager while doing so.

And this, to be honest, is what I want this book to be for you. The safe place, the game-changer, and the turning point. The place where you think, "Yes, it's do-able." Sometimes, we just need examples. Everyone is scared of change, and it's good to have a preview of what is to be expected. You see, life doesn't have to be black and white or absolutely wrong or right. I lived with this false assumption for the longest of time. But with time, I realised that nothing in this life is in absolute extreme. There are shades. Everything in this world that changes, goes through periods. Nothing in this life is abrupt. Look at the rising sun every day. It goes through a thousand shades before it shines brightly. A seed takes its time to turn into a plant. There is a flow in the movement of things; there is a pattern, and a momentum.

Everything is gradual. And so should be your *hijab*. It doesn't have to be perfect; it should, though, tell a story. A story of a strong girl who stood up for something that she believed in.

Nothing is stark or blunt in the matters of this world, and everything blends. And so should our religion and personality. They shouldn't be bipolar. They should be a well-blended mix of you and God. Only then will it be sustainable.

Further, if I would like you to learn one thing from this book, that would be: You and your *Deen* are not two things. They are one. Islam is not secular. Islam is all-inclusive. It is called a way of life for a reason. It has to have a flow. Not a rigid "my life and *Molvi Sahab*'s wife's life" contrast. When an artist learns to sketch, the biggest flaw he could have is the rigid outline that he gives to his drawings. For many art students, they would lose marks right there for the rigidity of their pencil work. Slowly, the student is taught to bring out the form by careful blending. It requires patience and tact until it starts to come out naturally. Such is the case with *hijab* and religion. It has to ease out, flow in your everyday life; it should come across as effortless, which, in fact, it is not. A lot of trial and error, a lot of going back and forth, and a lot of practice is what makes it flow naturally. And it's okay to mess up; it's okay to give it a shot and try again. I got it right the third time, and I am still a work in progress.

In this book, I have compiled all the ways that you can accommodate *hijab* in your life. I will walk you through the funny, the weird, and the cultural expectations of this world from a *hijabi*, and together we will figure out how to tackle each situation. For this matter, I have contacted numerous young ladies and professionals for insight so that it won't be my one-dimensional success story for you. You will be given an all-round view of things, keeping it very light and humorous from where you can pick out the points that work for you. Remember, I can do the research, and I can give you examples, but the assignment is on you. You have to figure out your life by yourself; I am merely a facilitator. You having this book in your hand today is a sign enough that you are curious about what this journey entails. Whatever stage you are on of a *hijab* lifestyle, whether on the absolute start, or you have been doing it for a while, you will definitely find some gems here to strengthen you on your journey, *Insha'Allah*.

The purpose of this book is not one-dimensional. Although it is written with the ultimate goal in mind—the *Akhirah*, it will unapologetically cater to all current issues in a young *Muslimah*'s life. Even though I have always loved to read all kinds of classic Islamic literature, none of them spoke about "me" as a person or my struggle in the real world. All of them spoke of an ideal *Muslimah*, to whom even after trying my best for twelve years, I am not even close. We will keep those texts close to our hearts to give us a goal, *Insha'Allah*, but first thing first—small steps. This book is all about small steps and little victories and those little speech bubbles in our heads that sound so un-Islamic. But by not addressing the problem, it will not go away. To have an identity of a *Muslimah* and have a successful professional life, let's do a little, but be firm on the little that we do.

In this book, I have tried to capture everything that goes on in a young person's mind. Every stage of life is like walking into the realm of Narnia; it seems fascinating, it's scary, and you don't know what is coming up next. It's exciting, but it's also petrifying. As a teenager, I have made a lot of mistakes. To be candid, let me say I had no guidance whatsoever. I had a huge generation gap with my parents, and no older person was around to advise or guide me. If I killed a person, I had no one to go to. What would you expect from such a teenager? Mistakes, right? And mistakes there were. Lots of them. I was all over the place. I was religious, I was emotional, and I was curious too. And since there was no one to answer my questions, most of the time I took on the quest myself to find the answers. And like I said before, the situations I landed myself in were not pretty. But Allah was there, and it was as if He kept me in a bubble. I bounced my way out every time, unhurt. That will be another topic that you will find me emphasising over and over again: your relationship with God. *Hijab* or no *hijab*, your relationship with Allah is of the utmost importance. That's the crux, the beginning, and the end. That's everything that is to this life. Once you have that, a lot of things will take shape automatically. You will find a relationship with Allah as an underlying theme in this book.

For this reason, precisely, in the next two chapters, we will discuss the more spiritual side of *hijab*. How do we know it's obligatory? What are the basics we should know? What about intention, and why are we doing it in the first place?

Once the basics are taken care of, we will move to the ornate and apparent side of it. How can you know what works for you? How to not get frustrated on bad *hijab* days? How can we make it more appealing, more girlie (or not), more me? Chapter 5 will tackle the questions which prevent *hijab* from becoming the natural part of you.

Then we will move on to the chapters talking about the psychological part, and some integral advice that I feel can benefit a girl being herself. It's never a good idea to give reins to other people about what you should be. It should be your decision, but also since *hijab* is an Islamic obligation, we do voluntarily or involuntarily become the ambassador of Islam once we wear it. Then, what's the best attitude to have? In Chapters 6–9, you will learn about the role of grit, dreams, positivity, indifference, empathy, and choice of words.

Chapter 10 deals with another important question: why do girls stop wearing *hijab*?

And Chapter 11 deals with the dos and don'ts in the

matters of love and infatuation.

This book is a cocktail of my experiences and observations. It's full of flashbacks of my teens and twenties, and of things that went right and things that didn't. It's a diary with a purpose. The purpose to help you through with that tug-of-war in the head. There is nothing more that I cherish than my *hijab*. I would never want to go back to my old headless-chicken confused days, and I want to save you all from that trouble too. It's a road worth travelling, and if I can make it any easier for you, it would be my absolute pleasure.

> We testify of what we have experienced and witnessed. May our testimony inspire others to share their story.
>
> — Lailah Gifty Akita

3

THE ULTIMATE CONNECTION

> Good communication is just as stimulating as black coffee, and just as hard to sleep after.
>
> —Anne Morrow Lindbergh

I am such a sucker for a good conversation. Nothing better than the right combination of intellect, humour, and knowledge. I am generally a quiet person, you see; it takes me a while to ease up to new people. But there are some with whom I am able to hit it off immediately. Most of my closest friends are those with whom I was able to ease into a conversation from the word "go." We'd laugh like hyenas (snorts and all), and they were able to get my dorky humour from day one. I never had to explain myself, and never had to defend my point of view. It is as it is, I am as I am, and they have loved me with all my flaws, which are, to be honest, quite a lot! Regardless of that, we have always gone home after meeting each other with huge smiles and the feeling of being understood.

And then there are those with whom I stumble on my words. I want to say something and end up saying something else. And then, to make it better, I try to explain myself, which makes me sound like a fool. Those conversations mostly end with "Sorry, I didn't mean to..." The worst thing is to explain the jokes. In my journal of life lessons (which is still in the form of mental notes), if someone doesn't get your humour, they don't get you at all. And in such cases, no matter how much I kick myself (in my head), the snowball effect of my awesomeness is out of control, making me look like a clown tumbling off the hill. Needless to say, I come back feeling defeated, misunderstood, and, in most cases, not liked.

The sad part is, in most cases, those people (who by now think I am either stuck-up or lack basic demeanour) might be the best of the people, but the lack of rapport generally leaves a gaping hole, and we as humans generally stick to the first impressions. There are always exceptions though; sometimes, we are able to see the other side of a person which went unnoticed the first time, and we are left pleasantly surprised. But generally, as sad as it sounds, the first impression remains the last impression.

I feel such is the case with our relationship with Allah سُبْحَانَهُ وَتَعَالَىٰ. I can't generalise, but as for myself, I have no memory of any active relationship or communication with Allah سُبْحَانَهُ وَتَعَالَىٰ while growing up. We had very static (and rather selective) *Gunah* and *Sawaab*, characterising our actions. We had very vivid pictures of *Jannah* and *Jahannum*, but no mention of Allah's ultimate *Rehmah* and why it is so important to build a relationship with Him.

Allah's سُبْحَانَهُ وَتَعَالَىٰ first introduction in Quran is:

بسم الله الرحمن الرحيم

"In the name of Allah, the Most Gracious, the Most Merciful."

Like I said, the first impression is the most important and the everlasting one. And the first impression Allah gives to whoever opens His Book is of a Merciful God.

What do you think He wants to instil in us before anything else?

What kind of a relationship does He want to initiate when we are assured from day one that His mercy overtakes everything?

In our social lives, won't we kill to have a relationship where we can be completely ourselves and are granted a ticket to mercy, compassion, and understanding regardless of our mistakes? We say *Bismillah* countless times in a day, but don't really comprehend what it signifies or inculcates in our subconscious. The importance of positive reinforcement and the power of positive words are a real deal. Research studies have shown multiple times that positive affirmations minimise anxiety, stress, and defensiveness, and keep us open to the idea that there is room for improvement. Until and unless we don't consciously realise what these words mean, we will be driven by fear rather than compassion.

Allah says in the Quran:

"Does He who created not know, while He is the Subtle, the All-Aware?" (67:14)

In simpler words, would He not know us, even though He created us in the first place?

Even though our parents gave birth to us, we can never truly be 100% ourselves in front of them. We always have a certain hesitation out of respect in front of our parents, no matter how kind and friendly they are. And our parents were even more so in front of their parents. As we go further down in history, we see that the parent-child equation was heavily dominated by respect, sometimes completely at the expense of understanding. We all have heard our elders say, "We could never say/act like this in front of our parents!"

The times are changing; children are much more open with their parents now. Parents too, are more aware and invested in their children these days. The overall family dynamics are much better than in previous times. Even then, we cannot say that a parent knows everything about their child.

It cannot in any way compare to the knowledge of Allah about His creation—the one who created us, our hearts, our thoughts, and who is continuously aware of what we go through in school, among friends; how our minds work, and what we think. It is impossible to hide anything from Him at all! In such a case, having an image of a God who is always judgemental would be detrimental to our self-worth. Yes, all our deeds are recorded, yes there is a law of reward and punishment, but it is most important to know that the One heading all these affairs is a Compassionate God.

Allah سُبْحَانَهُ وَتَعَالَى says in the Quran:

> "And when My servants ask you, concerning Me—indeed I am near. I respond to the invocation of the supplicant when he calls upon Me. So let them respond to Me [by obedience] and believe in Me that they may be [rightly] guided." (2:186)

This is the sweetest invitation to communication I've ever heard. I mean, who says I am always available? Except for someone who really, really loves us. If I take Allah's word on how I should see Him, it makes it so easy to be myself. He is my Lord who created me from scratch, who created the flaws that are in me, my humour, my personality, and my intellect. He created me in full, and in the best image. How can He not love me? Even with all my mistakes, with *hijab* or no *hijab*, He will love, accept, and forgive me. If there is not this surety, what's even the point then? When we create a small piece of art, we hang it proudly in our home. We love it regardless of all of its imperfect parts. Then how can we even think that Allah does not love us, His creation? With

His absolute sovereignty, His grandeur, and His absolute power, He wants us to know that He is near. Did He put a condition on us to be perfect before we reach out? Or to wear the *hijab* before it? No, He didn't. The call is for everyone! All we need to do is reach out.

You would be thinking why am I going on and on about building a relationship with Allah in a book about *hijab*. Because before we embark on the journey, we need to know why are we doing it in the first place. What is the *niyyah* (intention) behind it? And for whom? It says in a *Sahih Hadith*:

> *"Actions are but by intention and every man shall have but that which he intended. Thus he whose migration was for Allah and His messenger, his migration was for Allah and His messenger, and he whose migration was to achieve some worldly benefit or to take some woman in marriage, his migration was for that for which he migrated."* ~ *(Related by Bukhari and Muslim)*

The purpose of *hijab* is only one: to please Allah. It's one of the million ways in which He is protecting us, and we need to have blind faith on Him. If you start wearing *hijab* without having the right *niyyah*, or without building a relationship with Allah, the *hijab* won't sustain.

And to be honest, before taking up the *hijab*, my advice would be to build that relationship first! It will fix everything for you. Everything else branches out from this relationship—you and God. Everything else is secondary. Everything else is actually there to strengthen this relationship; even the prayer and the *hijab*. Good or bad, everything works for this relationship. Know without a doubt that He is there for everyone. For the *hijabis* and the non-*hijabis*, for the pious and the sinner—He is there. Always. Repeat it to yourself. HE IS THERE. HE IS THERE FOR THE IMPER-

FECT ME. THE REAL ME. Forever ready to listen to my whims and complaints, requests, and doubts and uncertainties. HE IS ALWAYS THERE. UNWAVERING.

So how do we build a relationship with Allah?

On a very basic level, I would just say, get to know Him. Talk to Him, speak to Him about everything. About your tiniest trouble. About the minutest heartache. I used to write letters to Him. Instead of Dear Diary, for me, it was *Dear Allah*. Now I kind of talk to Him anywhere I am, not imaginary, but real talks in my head. I present Him with my arguments. I ask Him please tell me what should I do now. I admit my mistakes. I confess about my shortcomings. Sometimes, it gets intense and I start talking loudly, to which my husband just rolls his eyes and thinks I am crazy. But you see, there doesn't have to be a right or a wrong way; you just have to start. As Brian Tracy said:

> *"Communication is a skill that you can learn. It's like riding a bicycle or typing. If you're willing to work at it, you can rapidly improve the quality of every part of your life."*

These are a few things you can do to build a relationship with him.

1. **Get to know Him (through Quran and His names and attributes):**

We can't really build a relationship with someone we don't know. And we certainly cannot love someone we have no idea about. Truth be told, that's the purpose of our creation: to shuffle through what life throws at us and find Allah *rab-bul izzat* in each of those events.

I ask you honestly, what do you know about your Creator except for what your mum told you?

Do you recognise His hand in each and everything you

do? If not, then there is definitely a communication gap. Your mind should be working like a decoder; everything that you see and everything that happens to you should connect you to Allah. It should be like, walking in the street, you spot a different-looking tree and you say, "It's the work of Allah *Al Musawwir* (The Fashioner)." You look at an ant and say, "Allah *Al Aleem* (The All-Knower) knows about every personality trait of this little one, and all his friends." Then you try to calculate how many ants, bugs, animals, and humans He has created, and HE knows each and every one of them personally; their personalities, desires, needs, past, and their present. This is called pondering. You learn about His names and qualities, and then you associate them with the things around you. The more you see, the more of Him you see.

I find this so enchanting, so liberating that He has given me the chance to understand Him. Me, a dot compared to the universe He has created. He lets me put the dots together, and whenever I am stuck, He takes my hand and guides me, and if I request something, He listens. Isn't this absolutely amazing? He is just so amazing. Amazing is actually a rather small word to describe Him. His grandeur is what fills up the heavens and the earth and what is within them. Once you know Him, there is no way your heart doesn't prostrate itself before Him every single minute of the day, merely by looking at the world around you.

> *The Prophet said: "Allah the Almighty said: I am as My servant thinks I am. I am with him when he mentions Me. If he mentions Me to himself, I mention him to Myself; and if he mentions Me in an assembly, I mention him in an assembly greater than it. If he draws near to Me a hand's length, I draw near to him an arm's length. And if he comes to Me walking, I go to him at speed." (Sahih Muslim)*

When you read the Quran, you find His names placed strategically, giving layers and layers of meaning to the *ayaah* it is placed in. The Quran is extremely profound as it is, and Allah's names are like jewels, giving depth to what is being said. They are there so we understand Him and His word (the Quran) in greater depth. All in a scheme of things, as in a map, each name is a password, a clue which takes us closer to Him. In simpler words, it is like a treasure hunt; to make sense of things you just need to get to the depth of the riddle, and every riddle is a door which takes you to another level. This is called being enlightened; the more you understand, the more the doors open and your heart is filled with light, amazement, and awe.

> *"Allah is the Light of the heavens and the earth. The example of His light is like a niche within which is a lamp, the lamp is within glass, the glass as if it were a pearly [white] star lit from [the oil of] a blessed olive tree, neither of the east nor of the west, whose oil would almost glow even if untouched by fire. Light upon light. Allah guides to His light whom He wills. And Allah presents examples for the people, and Allah is Knowing of all things." (Al Quran 24:35)*

2. Dua:

Talking to Him is what we call *dua* or invocation, where you call out to Allah to solve a problem for you. Do you know every time you make *dua*, however informal it may be, it is counted as a reward? Where in this world would you have such a reward system that you call out in desperation and it is counted in your favour. Prophet ﷺ said:

"Dua is the Essence of Ibadah" or *"Dua IS Ibadah."*

By making *dua*, we are actually making Allah our closest friend and ally. He already knows everything, but it's different when we initiate the conversation.

Growing up, *dua* for me was something mechanical that we do after the prayer or when we are in trouble. It lacked any real connection with Allah, but slowly when the relationship got better, so did the acceptance of *duas*. It has become a secret code; whenever I want something, He just gives it to me. It's crazy how sometimes I am craving for some food, and someone sends it to me out of the blue. I am dreaming of something, and it becomes a reality.

Dua to me is a saviour. I love how gooey, warm, and intense it feels. How, when I ask Allah for anything with the depth of my heart, He makes it come true. I have a habit of writing my *duas* every Ramadan, and believe me, whenever I take out my old *dua* lists, there is hardly any wish that didn't come true.

You see when a *dua* is manifested, more than the problem being solved, a person feels validated, and the *imaan* increases. The feeling is just too great when you feel that Allah listens to you. It grows you in conviction and love. And makes the plunge of faith easy for you.

Tips for getting your duas answered

I learnt these tips from Sheikh Mohammad al Shareef, and I owe him my life for teaching me these little hacks.

a. ***Make a dua list:*** I generally do this yearly in Ramadan, and review it on the 1st of January to see how far along I have come. It also serves as a New Year's resolution and gives me clarity of what I want in the coming year.

b. ***Repeat them with passion:*** Repeat, repeat, and repeat! Like that child who won't take no for an answer. That's the determination we need. Ask and don't stop. If nothing else, you are earning *hasanat* every step of the way.

c. ***Mention Allah's appropriate name with your duas:*** When do you get a better response: when you call someone with their real name or with their "special" name? I feel special names ooze of association and closeness, like you know someone more than others. It is the etiquette of *dua*, and is a condition of fulfilling of a *dua*. I really feel calling Allah with His different names adds colour and depth to the *dua*.

d. *Make the same dua for others:* Prophet ﷺ said, *"No Muslim servant supplicates for his brother behind his back but that the angel says: And for you the same." (Sahih Muslim)* Make *dua* for others, and you won't have to ask anything for yourself ever again!

e. *Avoid sins, especially haram deeds.* When you stop yourself from something that you want to just out of His love, He will provide for you out of appreciation of this gesture.

f. *Ask as much as you want, even the little things which sound silly:* Companions of the Prophet ﷺ used to ask Allah even if their shoelace was broken. No *dua* is silly. It is all about the absolute belief that He will provide. We just need to hang in there.

g. *Don't say "Insha'Allah" in your dua:* *Insha'Allah* means "if you will." In *dua*, we say *Ameen*, which means "May it be (exactly) like this!" Have the ultimate faith and say, "Oh Allah, make it happen!" And have the faith that Allah has all the power in the world to make it happen for you in the best way possible.

h. *Have firm belief that Allah will accept.* It is His promise that He will! And He fulfils all His promises.

i. *Know that dua is the greatest of worships,* and that Allah loves it when we ask of Him and only Him, and no one but Him.

3. Have friends who remind you of Allah

We humans are quite impressionable; we adapt very quickly. If you have people around you who don't believe, it would be harder for you to believe. It's as simple as that. When everyone is doing the same thing, it naturally becomes very easy. Faith can be learnt. Have friends who are higher in faith to keep you motivated and keep you fresh with the idea of how to keep the connection strong.

Good deeds and relationship with Allah go in circles, one strengthening the other. Any good deed that you do leads to a better relationship with Allah سُبْحَانَهُ وَتَعَالَى; the better the relationship, the more *taufeeq* to do good deeds. In the matter of *imaan*, we grow in spirals. But if the base of the spiral is not strong, the tower will fall. The base is the communication, and the desired is His pleasure; in the middle are the matters of this world which we have to navigate as per the instructions in the Quran and *Sunnah*.

Keep the communication strong, and the spiral will come naturally.

I wish you a happy ride upward!

> **The single biggest problem in communication is the illusion that it has taken place.**
>
> —George Bernard Shaw

4

STRENGTHENING THE CORE

> If you know where you are from, it is harder for people to stop you where you are going.
>
> —Matshona Dhliwayo

The first time I started wearing the *hijab*, I was in Grade 9. Back then, I don't think I had actually grasped the meaning of what *hijab* really means. I just took it up because I saw some of my friends wearing it. I never asked why they did it. I just found it a very "pure" thing to do. A thing that a "good" girl would do. Our uniform was the most hideous. A typical school in Pakistan would have a nice straight-cut shirt with a *shalwar* and *dupatta*, but no, our school tried to be innovative and failed badly. We had a half-sleeved, pleated frock in blue-and-white checked cloth, with a belt on the waist, a breast pocket, applet loops for the *dupatta* to go in, and a *shalwar* to go with it. Everything they thought was fashionable; they put it together, and the outcome was horrendously wrong. To top it all, I decided to be pious all of a sudden, without having the full knowledge of what that entails, and I pleaded with my mum to buy a huge black triangular scarf with a thick lace on the sides, because that's what everyone was wearing, and I had no originality (but of course!). If I would be my mum, I would quietly be chuckling at what my child was trying to achieve, and would patiently wait for her to come back to her senses in her own time, and this is exactly what my mum did.

I started going to school with that attire of a clown. Mind you, the sleeves of the school uniform were half, and I didn't think it was a problem (speaks volumes about my knowledge of the subject, doesn't it!). The moment I'd come home, my *hijab* would land in a corner, not to see the light of the day again, until the next school day. All events, social gatherings, and extended family get-togethers were without any *hijab* and mostly in very tiny sleeves, as was the fashion of that time. This idiocy lasted for a good few months. I don't know what put me off it, but whatever it was I am utterly grateful.

This was the story of my first try on *hijab*. I had no sense of purpose, and I had no knowledge; of course, it was bound to fail. I am just glad that I didn't grow up as clueless as I was. There is nothing detrimental to a religion or a cause with people without knowledge representing that cause. And that, my dear friends, is exactly what I was. And for this reason, I feel it's important to educate the masses about what exactly *hijab* is, and why we have to do it in the first place.

This chapter will basically serve as the appendix for *hijab* diction. From here on, hopefully, you will have a much clearer view of the actual requirement of *hijab* in Islam. I'll try to make it as easy and fun as I can, but this is real important information, you guys. If you are thinking of wearing the *hijab*, or are just curious about it, know that the points I am discussing here are the crux, the base, and the core of the matter.

1. **Where does it say that women have to cover their hair?**

Well, it says so in clear words in the Quran. The exact words are:

يَا أَيُّهَا النَّبِيُّ قُل لِّأَزْوَاجِكَ وَبَنَاتِكَ وَنِسَاءِ الْمُؤْمِنِينَ يُدْنِينَ عَلَيْهِنَّ مِن جَلَابِيبِهِنَّ ۚ ذَٰلِكَ أَدْنَىٰ أَن يُعْرَفْنَ فَلَا يُؤْذَيْنَ ۗ وَكَانَ اللَّهُ غَفُورًا رَّحِيمًا ─
سورة الأحزاب- الآية: 59

> *O Prophet, tell your wives and your daughters and the women of the believers to bring down "over" themselves [part] of their outer garments. That is more suitable that they will be known and not be abused. And ever is Allah Forgiving and Merciful. (33:59)*

2. **Why is it only for women?**

Actually, it's for both men and women. There are two *ayahs* in the Quran regarding the *hijab*, the first one is about men, and the next one about women. So, in context, men are ordered to cover up and guard their eyes first, rather than the women.

> *Tell the believing men to lower their gaze and guard their private parts. That is purer for them. Indeed, Allah is Acquainted with what they do. (Al Quran 24:30)*

> *And tell the believing women to lower their gaze and guard their private parts and not expose their adornment except that which [necessarily] appears thereof and to wrap [a portion of] their headcovers over their chests and not expose their adornment except to their husbands, their fathers, their husbands' fathers, their sons, their husbands' sons, their brothers, their brothers' sons, their sisters' sons, their women, that which their right hands possess, or those male attendants having no physical desire, or children who are not yet aware of the private aspects of women. And let them not stamp their feet to make known what they conceal of their*

> *adornment. And turn to Allah in repentance, all of you, O believers, that you might succeed. (Al Quran 24:31)*

Allah created men and women for different purposes. The man was given more strength and the woman was given more love and sensitivity. Even though we are living in times of gender equality, one cannot deny that in jobs that require labour work, like in the construction industry, men are better suited. And where compassion is most needed, like Montessori teachers, women are a better match. If you look at movies of older times, you will see men working in heat with only the lower part covered, while women are shown in long dresses, however poor they may be. Why? Because if men were in their skirts, it would be impossible for them to do the work that they are built to do; besides, a woman is much more beautiful than a man is, and like it or not, we do need the protection that Allah is offering us. The difference of dressing is to guard the beauty of women, to protect the men and the women from becoming a victim of their own desires, and to serve the practicality of how each of us is made. Remember the book *Men Are from Mars and Women Are from Venus*? We actually are different species and need to be treated as such.

3. **But why? What purpose does it serve if I cover myself or not?**

The simplest answer is, prevention is better than cure.

The simplest example is of COVID-19. In the COVID situation all around the world, each person is responsible to protect themselves. But they are also responsible for society as a whole. If they don't adhere to the rules laid out by the Government and blame others, do you think the system will work? No. Each one has to do their part to protect themselves and the other. That's how it can be a safe space for everyone. You live your life, do things that you have to do but through the proper protocol. Similar is the case with the Islamic dress code.

Moral degeneration is the epidemic of our times. Abortions, rape, sexual abuse, and extra-marital affairs are in the headlines every day. How did we come to this? I don't want to sound dramatic, but simple rules and values are there for a reason. They keep us within the boundaries. If our parents lay the rule of "you have to be back home by *Maghrib*," we may argue and say, "My parents don't trust me. They don't think I am old enough to handle this," but there is a reason why they are doing it; they have been through our age, and they do know what can go wrong.

Similarly, there are some ground rules set by Allah. He knows the damage our desires can do for us. A heart, especially a young heart, is like a wild horse; it has too many hormones and no reins. It shouldn't be left unguarded, or it might hurt itself and others. The purpose of *hijab* is to close all doors, which can lead to sexual desires. Like a mask in the COVID situation. We need to trust Him on this.

In a society where a woman covers and both men and women lower their eyes, the chances for illicit relationships or sexual misconduct go down drastically. But the thing is, rules can be written down but can't be forced. If rules are forced, people find ways to break the rules anyway. The following of the code only comes from within. It only works if you have complete trust in the system and the Being who invented the system in the first place. If not, then men will never lower their eyes, and women will never adhere to the dress code; each one will blame the other. The following of the code can only happen when you have *taqwa* in your heart. When you are conscious of Allah's presence, even if your eye falls on someone and you really like them too, you will keep yourself in control. And if it really means a lot to you, you will find a way to go through the proper channel.

4. Why does only Islam as a religion pay so much attention to modesty? Why not other religions?

Not only Islam, but every religion has respected modesty.

The two other major monotheistic religions Judaism and Christianity share almost identical views on modesty as Islam. Quoting from My Jewish Learning and Jewish Virtual Library:

> *"Modesty is the foundation of Jewish values and is one of the fundamental underpinnings of a Jewish family. It is popularly thought to apply primarily to women, but it is a desirable quality in men as well. Tzniut in Hebrew means modesty, simplicity, a touch of bashfulness, and reserve."*

"In the *Talmud (Berakhot 24a),* the rabbis define hair as sexually erotic *(ervah)* and prohibit men from praying in sight of a woman's hair.

> *"It is not customary for a Jewish woman to go to the marketplace with only a head covering, and it is required for her to have her bodied covered with something like her wedding garment, like a shawl, a husband is obliged to provide this for her."*

And quoting from the Holy Bible

> *"I also want the women to dress modestly, with decency and propriety, adorning themselves, not with elaborate hairstyles or gold or pearls or expensive clothes, but with good deeds, appropriate for women who profess to worship God." (Timothy 2:9, 10)*

> *"While the heart is the primary issue, the Bible also teaches that we are to be conscious of the shamefulness of public nakedness (i.e., being improperly or insufficiently clothed). God's standards of proper*

attire are demonstrated throughout the Scriptures from Genesis chapter three to Jesus' own clothing. They teach clearly that attire matters, and modesty, both inward and outward, are an essential aspect of the Christian life." (quoted from Gospel Broadcasting Network, The Truth about Modesty)

Interestingly enough, all these three religions recount the event of eating from the forbidden tree and exposure of the private parts of Prophet Adam and Hawaa (peace be upon them) in almost identical language:

"And Adam and his wife ate of it, and their private parts became apparent to them, and they began to fasten over themselves from the leaves of Paradise. And Adam disobeyed his Lord and erred." (Al-Qur'an 20:121)

All leaning towards the same message that sinning leads to a lack of *hayaa* (modesty).

If you read up on all the sources I mentioned above, you will see an uncanny resemblance in the concepts of modesty in these three religions.

The only difference is that some cultures have abandoned these teachings while others haven't, but in all the religions, there are conservative minorities who still stick to the basics.

5. Do we ONLY have to cover the hair?

No, a woman is supposed to cover anything which can enlighten her feminine beauty, which includes her hair, her chest, the shape of her waist and legs. It also includes avoiding too much makeup, which enhances the face and makes it difficult for a man to look away. Some scholars believe that a woman should be covered from head to toe, including face, hands, and feet; others believe it's okay to show the face (devoid of makeup) and hands. Both opinions have very strong evidence from hadith. In any case, both schools of thought believe that if you fear there is *fitnah*, then you must cover your face as well.

Hijab also entails avoiding any seductive or flirtish gestures, like talking in a seductive voice or unnecessarily laughing or giggling with the non-*mehrams*.

The same applies to men; they have to cover their *aurah*—that is, the navel to the knee—at all times. And they are also not allowed to flirt with women, seduce them, shake hands with them, or touch them in any other manner.

In addition to this, women are to cover themselves from other women from the navel to the knee at all times. In actuality, neck-down to the knee should be covered, but the strictest ruling is navel to the knee. The men too have to cover themselves from the navel to knee around other men at all times.

- *Aurah* or *satr*, in Islamic terminology, refers to intimate parts of the human body, which must be covered by clothing, and revealing it is sinful.

- The exceptions of *aurah* can only be made in medical conditions.

6. What is the concept of mehram in the matter of hijab?

Mehram is anyone whom you are permanently forbidden to marry because of blood ties, marriage ties, and ties of breastfeeding. A woman does not need to cover her hair when she is in the presence of these males of her family.

Through blood ties, *mehrams* include the following:

- Parents, grandparents, and further ancestors.

- Children, grandchildren, and further descendants.

- Siblings of parents and grandparents.

- Siblings and children of siblings.

Through marriage ties, *mehrams* can be the following:

- Husband.
- Father-in-law, mother-in-law, son-in-law, and daughter-in-law.
- Step-father (if the marriage is consummated).
- Step-mother (even if the marriage is not consummated).
- Step-son (husband's son) (even if the marriage is not consummated).
- Step-daughter (wife's daughter) (if the marriage is consummated).

Through *rada* (breastfeeding), mehrams are as below:

- If a child is breastfed by anyone other than his or her mother, all the above relatives of the *rada* parents become *mehram*.

The list seems lengthy, but once you get the hang of it, it becomes easy. It was important for me to mention all the details so that a reader doesn't get half-baked knowledge. There are gradations of *hijab* within the *maharim* (plural of *mehram*), even though there is a whole list of *maharim*, but a husband is the only one who is allowed to be intimately close to a girl and vice versa. Apart from that, a girl is supposed to be in decent clothes even when among the *maharim*, meaning you can't be in see-through or revealing clothes in the presence of a brother or father just because they are immediate family.

7. **What is the difference among burqa, hijab, abaya, and jilbaab? I can't seem to wrap my head around so many terminologies.**

These are all different names for the kind of coverings Muslim women use. *Hijab* actually is the Arabic term for "cover," based on the root meaning "to veil, cover, screen, and shelter." The word *hijab* today is used as a general term for a headscarf, but it refers to general modesty—which can be achieved in many ways.

I hope this illustration helps clear the confusion.

Niqab A veil covering the head and face, but not the eyes, usually worn with an abaya.	**Hijab** A general term meaning "to cover" or "veil" most commonly refers to a headscarf that covers the hair and neck, but not the face.	**Burka** An enveloping over-garment that covers the entire body and face, with a mesh panel across the eyes allowing the wearer to see in front of her.	**Chador** A full-length open cloak commonly worn by Iranian women, typically held closed in the front by the wearer's hands or under their arms.

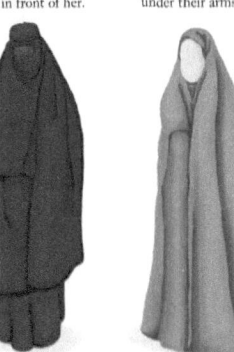

Khimar A headcovering that comes down till wrists. It covers the head, shoulders, chest and arms.	**Dupatta** A long scarf loosely draped across the head and shoulders, common in south Asia and often paired with matching shalwar kameez.	**Jilbaab** A loose fitted outer covering. It covers the wearer from head to toe.	**Abaya** The abaya is a simple, loose robe-like over-t garment, traditional in black color. It can be worn with the niqāb, or hijab.

Illustration by Tashna Salim

Whatever way a Muslim woman decides to dress herself, the point is the same: modesty.

8. Can I wear a wig to cover my hair?

No. The purpose of *hijab* is to cover and protect all aspects of female beauty, not to layer it. If your mum says, "There is food in the kitchen, go cover it before some fly lands on it," you can't top it up with more food and call it covering, can you? The same is the case with *hijab*, you have to cover, not warp.

Though interestingly enough, in Jewish culture, it is allowed. They call these wigs or *sheitel*.

9. Is hijab more important, or being a good person is? Why can't I just be a good Muslim without wearing hijab?

Think of our *Deen* Islam as an exam paper. The coursebook is Quran and *Hadith*; how to answer the questions is demonstrated in the *Seerah*. In the question paper (which is our life), there are individual questions that need to be answered. Each question has its merit and marks. The highest marks are for answers closest to the concepts taught in the coursebook. The more and the better you fill-up the paper, the higher the marks you will get.

If a person wears a *hijab*, she gets marks for it. But if this *hijabi* does not pray, she loses marks in a different way. If a person prays but tells lies, they lose marks in another way.

Quran and *Sunnah* have given us the best examples to follow. That is the ultimate merit criteria. That's what we should ultimately aim to achieve. But we are all humans, and everyone has their strengths and weaknesses. What is easy for you may be hard for someone else. So there is no THIS or THAT. There is no comparison. We need to have passing marks in all the subjects, be it prayer, hijab, truthfulness, or any other matter of faith. The point is not to compare the questions but to fill them up according to the best of our capability, get good marks, and make it to the merit list.

10. Someone mocked me for wearing hijab AND listening to music. I don't like it.

It seems like a simple question, but it isn't. It's rather a multidimensional question. You see, when a person wears *hijab*, others somehow consider them as higher than others. She might not necessarily be, but that's how she is seen. It's the same as you are wearing a T-shirt with your country's name on it. If you do something nice, people who may not even know you would say, "a Pakistani girl did such a marvellous thing," but if you get into a fight, however right you may be, a spectator would report, "I saw a Pakistani fighting in the middle of the road, saying this and that." In both scenarios, the person became a representative without even realising it. Like it or not, we all represent our country, our *Deen,* and our family every day. It's an invisible flag that we carry; it's an honour and a responsibility at the same time. When a girl decides to wear a *hijab* or a boy decides to have a long beard, they kind of give colour to that invisible flag. They are noticed more, praised more, and criticised more.

Now in reference to the question, since listening to music is considered *haram* in Islam as it takes one away from the remembrance of Allah, there may be many other girls who do listen to it, but you, in particular, were pointed out because of the tiny flag that you carry because of your *hijab*. I would not say that it is right to judge a person, but generalising is a system built in us to identify and quicken the processing that happens in the mind. People can't help but generalise; that's how we are made. This is how we form someone's first impressions. It's a more psychological process than a conscious one. But one must completely avoid judging others consciously or voice any thought that may hurt another person.

On another note, it is important to identify a sin as a sin and to know and differentiate right from wrong. If we don't keep that distinction, our morals will dwindle. But it is the sin that we should dislike and not the person. Because people commit sin; we all do. Just because someone has sinned differently, they shouldn't be mocked, AND it's not our job to judge.

We can't change other people, but we can change how we process these things. First of all, when it happens, smile and move on. You have to answer to Allah, not to others. But do remember that you are carrying that tiny flag with you. But if you are in a similar position where you find yourself judging another person, you have to know these things:

- Call a sin a sin (not verbally, but in your mind) just so it doesn't become a normality to you.

- Don't judge that person. It's not your job; it's Allah's. You don't know what her other good deeds are.

- Don't ever taunt or smirk or in any way make the other person feel bad.

- If you can, teach by example. Not by indirect stories, or by WhatsApp messages out of the blue. People get the vibe of being judged, and they back off very quickly. If you want to correct someone, approach the matter very carefully. The job here is not to make a person feel bad but to stop her from sinning.

I hope I have answered the basic questions that you might need when starting the journey. I haven't gone into too much detail (though I was itching to do so), but these are the basic facts that every Muslim and preferably the non-Muslim should know. It is general knowledge. Every religion takes care of their women. It shouldn't be taken as an offence, but rather consider it an honour that the Creator of the Worlds has given as a thoughtful plan for our treatment. It speaks of what a loving and Compassionate God we have. Fathers are the most protective of their daughters; no one can dare raise an eyebrow at their girl when they are present. Then how can we think that Allah the most Compassionate would not be protective of us?

The *hijab* is a story of love, protection, grace, and piety, and it should not be taken any lesser than that.

> **As women, we will never reach true liberation until we stop trying to mimic men and value the beauty in our own God given distinctiveness.**
>
> —YASMIN MOGAHED

5

I LOOK HORRIBLE

> Style is a way to say who you are without having to speak.
>
> — RACHEL ZOE

I remember the night before I took the *hijab*, the final night after which there hasn't been any turning back, *Alhamdulillah*. I and a *hijabi* friend of mine went out for a dinner. I remember my mind was made up. Almost. The heart was on to it, but the doubts were giving their last shot. The purpose of the meeting was also the same—to talk about all the fears and insecurities and to seal the deal once and for all. We spoke about *hijab* at length, and I was convinced that I was taking the leap! But right before we were leaving the restaurant, I stopped in my tracks and said, "But what about my *saris*? All my backless blouses and beautiful *saris*! Will I never be able to wear them again?" A sudden surge of nostalgia gripped me. And I was ready to throw away the whole night's discussion for the love of my wardrobe; to which my friend said, "Kiran, now you are just giving way to *waswaas* (whispers) of *shaitan*. Now you have no reason to back out." And that shut me up right there.

The struggle is real, guys. One day you are a good-looking girl with your hair perfectly framing your face; the next day you decide to wear a *hijab* and end up looking like an egg. I will not sugar-coat it for you. I had three trials on *hijab*, and believe me, the initial period was the same. Absolutely and inconsolably uncomfortable. I didn't feel like myself; the person looking back at me from the mirror was a badly dressed stranger who didn't know how to pin her scarf.

But the good thing is that you come around it. Once the decision is made, which is the most difficult part, you do find your way through it. The battle is never easy; even when you are 100% convinced. You are basically giving up a part of yourself. And it is never possible without faith. Faith is the name of the game in the end. As liberating as it is for me or any other *hijabi*, the first few months are a true test of faith. Like they say for any skill, the only way out is through; it applies equally to the first few months of *hijab*.

I started my *hijab* journey in jeans and long-sleeved shirts. It served the purpose and gave me the initial kick. But it really didn't cover the shape of my body properly, for which I got scolded by my mum often. And she was right; first things first. The purpose is not to wrap but to cover. Slowly, I moved towards long shirts with loose pants and *dupattas*, or loose *kurtis* with jeans with bigger *sheilas*. It would look fashionable, demure, and smart. But as I studied the Quran, soon it wasn't enough for me, and I took up *abaya*. And have been on it since. I do go back and forth on the makeup front, to be honest, but the *abaya* has stuck with me, and it is where I truly find my peace. It is so strange that once I used to worry about my *saris*; today, I wouldn't want it any other way.

It was exciting in the start, terrifying in the middle, and then it started to get easy. I mean, *abaya* is the easiest way to look regal in a matter of minutes. It's a one-size-fits-all kind of attire; going to the park: *abaya*, going to a party: *abaya*, going to a wedding: *abaya*, going to a funeral: *abaya*!

It has saved me so much money and time. I don't have to worry about curling or straightening my hair anymore, or worrying about what to wear. Especially when I am running late, which surprisingly happens very often. So yes, *abaya* has been a true friend.

It's something on the lines of what President Obama said:

> *"You'll see I wear only grey or blue suits. I'm trying to pare down decisions. I don't want to make decisions about what I'm eating or wearing. Because I have too many other decisions to make."*

Since I generally go around my day making many important decisions, like what to eat for breakfast, before lunch, after lunch, before dinner, and after dinner, I happily took half the advice and made myself a happy woman!

My two cents that I can concur from my various attempts at *hijab* are given below:

1. **Start Slow:**

Get comfortable with covering your heard first. Start with little but firm steps. Slowly start covering your head and see how you feel; try it when you are going alone to the mall or somewhere, where people don't really know you. Once you gain a bit of confidence, go big. Some of my friends started with a casual drape on their heads with half their hair showing. It wasn't perfect, but believe me, even that was a struggle, and slowly they too took steps forward and never looked back.

Though it works differently for each, you know what would work for you. Some go for the jackrabbit start. They start big and proper. For them, it's now or never. If it works for you, good for you. But I am a believer in testing the waters first; find your grounding and then take the leap. Slow and firm. The pace of the tortoise is definitely the winning pace. It won't exhaust or overwhelm you. Remember that Allah loves the acts which are continuous no matter how small.

> *The Messenger of Allah said, "Take up good deeds only as much as you are able, for the best deeds are those done regularly even if they are few." (ibn majah)*

2. **Experiment:**

Experiment with different styles until you reach the one that works the best for you. It is most important to feel comfortable in what you wear, and to feel "You." Confidence comes with both comfort and style that you feel as your own. Experiment, experiment, and experiment—until you feel right. It might take a while. But the key is not to be impatient. I recently gave this advice to someone, which helped her immensely. I would say the same here: give it at least six months. Try different styles and fabrics and see what works, but I would advise not to invest heavily initially. I bought many long-sleeved shirts and silken scarves only to adopt the *abaya* a few months later; a lot of clothes were wasted. The silken scarves gave me a headache and were the hardest to manage. I resorted to cotton scarves and lighter *sheilas* later. My daughter likes the stretchy scarves which don't need any pins, etc. It's easy to maintain for a young girl with a sporty look, and there is no hassle of caps and pins. You can buy a few of each kind or borrow them from a friend to see what you feel the most comfortable with. Once you work out what suits you the most, you can work towards making a collection.

3. **Lay low initially:**

Danielle Isaac says the following in her article, "When to Lay Low versus Take Action."

> *Just as in nature, there are seasons in our own lives. We experience natural ebbs and flows. In the winter, many things go dormant to prepare for rapid new growth in the Spring. This period of rest and darkness is crucial to the success of the new season… You need to prepare for your Spring. This is a good thing. Trust it rather than judge it. Relax and know that lying dormant is sometimes the best thing you can do to prepare for rapid growth.*

I would highly recommend treating your experimenting period as the "preparation of the spring." It doesn't mean that you stop meeting people; just avoid huge gatherings initially. Try to time your experimenting period away from any weddings in the family, prom at the school, graduation party, etc. Such big events are the worst when you are still working on your style. Maybe you are strong enough to go for it and make a statement; if you are, go make a star of yourself! But if you are not, I would really ask you to give it some time. Experimenting in front of a large crowd may not help with the confidence. You are already struggling with a new self-image, and criticism can really hurt the process. I remember I was still new to this journey when my sister got married. First of all, even after trying my best, I couldn't look as good as I wished. To me, everyone looked better than me, while I struggled to keep the scarf on my head with a toddler. I still cringe when I see my pictures of such an important event in my life. Second, every Tom, Dick, and Harry had an opinion on why I should not cover my head, whether covering of the head is even mentioned in the Quran, that my *hijab* wasn't 100% *Sharia*-compliant, et cetera, et cetera.

And seriously, hardly any of them were pleasant. It was really bad, I tell you. I was angry and frustrated. I wouldn't wish it for any of you.

So my advice: try to lay low until you find your grounding, and once you find your ground, walk the path like a princess and inspire those around you while wearing the *ayaah* of the Quran. The confidence comes when you know what you are doing. Give it that time. It will all pay off well, I promise.

4. Take up like-minded friends:

A support system is necessary to give you the required footing. You need people who are in the same boat or have been through it. As I told you in the initial chapter, it was my friend's confidence and style that inspired me. Having strong, like-minded friends is a virtue held high in our religion as well.

> *The Prophet ﷺ said, "A man is upon the religion of his best friend, so let one of you look at whom he befriends." (Tirmidhi)*

Not only in religion, but in recent success studies, the concept of building yourself up with like-minded people is much esteemed. Napoleon Hill, author of the successful book *Think and Grow Rich*, calls it **"the Mastermind group."** A Mastermind group is a grouping of peers who support each other in achieving their goals. All participants grow beyond themselves by challenging each other, brainstorming ideas, and helping and believing in each other.

> *No two minds ever come together without, thereby, creating a third, invisible, intangible force which may be likened to a third mind.*
>
> — NAPOLEON HILL

Having the right friends at such an important phase in your life can make or break you. If the crowd you hang out with, already looks down at people covering their heads, there is no way you can extract confidence from them for this purpose. I am not asking to give up on your friendships, but just find girls who are on the same journey as you are alongside. It will help with finding your way through, and in finding your grounding.

5. **Seek inspiration:**

Look up to the *hijabi* bloggers. Ten years back, there weren't half of the social media that we have today, let alone the amazing *hijabi* bloggers and influencers. There are so many *hijab* tutorials available today. So many success stories that the heart fills up with warmth. We know that there are many who are walking the same struggles as we are, and they are ready to help us without even knowing us. So many styles, all broken down in easy-to-follow step-by-step guides. It's a blessing for the newbies.

You can make a Pinterest board and pin all the images that you like. You can search online, and before you know it, Instagram and Google will be throwing images at you (thank you, intelligent advertising!). Look for what seems to be your style and grow from there.

6. **Consider the lifestyle of the place you are in:**

I generally like wearing long *abayas*, but when I go back to Pakistan, it is impossible to do so. By the end of the day, the ends of my *abaya* are full of dirt. Hence, I have to take slightly shorter ones to Pakistan. In Paris, I wore a long one, which was all wet from the rainwater in no time. In all my pictures, I have a knot at the end of my *abaya* to prevent my pants and shoes from getting wet. As important as it is to look good, so is the climate and circumstance of the place you are at. You also have to consider your workplace and the weather. When travelling to Florida, I took a few jersey dresses so I could have a few decent pictures taken in my new wardrobe, but it was so hot that by the end of the trip, I was wearing my worn-out casual black *abaya*.

If you don't dress for comfort, you won't be able to carry on for long. Don't crowd your closet, but do keep a few outfits for every occasion. A few formal ones, a few sporty ones for outdoor activities, a few smart casuals for work, etc., and a few for travelling.

> Just remember that ultimately dressing is all about attitude, feeling comfortable, and confident.
>
> —Kate Moss

7. **Stay true to yourself:**

In the end, stay true to yourself and your purpose. Don't try to copy someone else's style as it is. There is a difference between copying and taking inspiration. It's a big job you are taking upon yourself; don't start off on a shaky ground by not being yourself. The power of personal style goes beyond what the eye sees. You have to feel it to convey it. Vibes don't lie; if you are not at home with what you wear, it will convey itself one way or the other. If you feel you don't look good, it will show in your manner. By that, I don't mean to overdo anything, but to NOT overdo anything! Be yourself. Be unapologetically yourself. Feel good. Feel damn good to be wearing the *ayaah* of the Quran every day. And do so while feeling beautiful every day. That's the only way to stick to such a big change in your life.

> If you are not comfortable in your own skin, you
> won't be comfortable in your own clothes.
>
> —Iris Apfel

8. Remember why you are doing it in the first place:

As important as it is to stay true to yourself, and to be relevant in these fast-paced times, don't forget why you are doing it in the first place. Don't forget that every time you cover yourself up modestly, you are pleasing Allah and gaining rewards. Don't pollute that by trying to impress people. They will be impressed anyway when you are sure of yourself and your purpose. Everything comes in its own time. You should trust that and remain firm on your cause.

> "O Children of Adam! We have bestowed clothings upon you to cover yourselves and as an adornment; and the clothing of taqwa (Allah consciousness), that is BEST. Such are among the Ayat (signs) of Allah, that they may remember." (Surah Al-A'raf 7:26)

Know that there will be good days and bad. You might feel beautiful one day, and the next day, you want to throw the scarf away, sit in a corner, and cry. But know that you will get through. Know that you are strong, and Allah is with you in this every step of the way. You will find your way, style, and grit. Stick to your vision; the rest will eventually fall in its place. May Allah be with you in this endeavour.

> A personal style is like handwriting—it
> happens as the by-product of our own way of
> seeing things, enriched by the experiences of
> everything around us.
>
> —Massimo Vignelli

6

THE GRIT

> God honours a beautiful blend of gift and grit!
> He gives the gift, and He expects us to have
> the grit to practice and learn how to use it
> effectively.
>
> —BETH MOORE

How do you imagine a motivational book writer to be?

To me, this is what she looks like: A disciplined person who wakes up early in the morning and has a healthy breakfast which probably consists of some eggs, fruits, jam, fancy bread, and orange juice (I somehow cannot imagine her without her morning orange juice). She'd have the first meal of the day on the porch of her beautiful home basking in the morning sun in an immaculately ironed blue-and-white-striped skirt and a crisp white cotton blouse. (As you can see, I spend a commendable amount of my time on Instagram.) After which she calmly reaches out to her laptop and writes. Taking pauses to look at the vast *Downton Abbey* look-alike garden in front of her, she smiles her poised smiles when she writes something funny in her Jane

Austen-styled wit.

Now that you have already spent money buying my book, let me tell you I am nothing like the image above! First of all, I would never want you to know the clothes in which I am writing such an important book on *hijab*. Pyjamas are my friend, and any criticism against them would be taken seriously. Second, I love to sleep till late whenever I can! My kids know it, and they have accepted their fate. Also, I love to have breakfast in bed, but since my family hasn't yet realised what a successful writer I am going to be, they don't treat me as such. Even when my husband is ever so kind to get it for me, it's nothing like you see in the movies and it certainly doesn't have a glass of juice in it. And if I would have jam and bread every day, I would look like a cow (so boiled eggs, please!). When I am on a holiday, I do try and mimic the writer of my dreams.

I am averagely disciplined, averagely skilled, averagely talented, and I am fear-stricken at the start of almost all my big projects. But one thing, the one thing that should make you have faith in me is my passion! Here is another spoiler alert again: I am not like one of those round-the-clock-passionate and driven people. My passion hits me like lightning. It's hard to explain what it is like. It's like I am blinded once it hits me. Like one minute I would be lazing in my bed, and the next minute it would be hard for me to breathe. It comes like a wave, like a vision, and then it doesn't let me rest. And it can be as random as a balloon in the pool. It won't be extraordinary for others, but it makes my adrenaline go high up!

Take the idea for writing this book as an example. I was in Walmart, quickly picking up snacks right before a road trip, while the rest of the family was in the car impatiently waiting. I saw a book, liked the title, and picked it up. It was a light read, not an exceptionally amazing one, but refreshing. That's when, all of a sudden, it came to me, "When I write a book, it would be light but inspirational!" And while I read the book, I kept on making mental notes, "My book will be this and this!" "I like her honesty! My book would be honest too." I was so excited about all those ideas I had, which were inspired by that book. That book was not even remotely close to mine, but while reading it, it was like I was thunderstruck; ideas kept on coming in like uninvited guests. And I didn't know what to do with them. I was on a vacation and had few exhibitions lined up when I'd get home. Plus, I had no idea how the book market worked. Once back home, my focus shifted away for a few months, but wow, the Law of Attraction—what a deliciously exciting *nae'mah* (blessing) of Allah it is! I landed face-to-face with the publishing company whose free workshop I had attended two years back. I didn't have any ideas then, but I had ideas now. I didn't have the finances and resources then, which I had now. Such is the timing of the Amazing Planner, the *Al Mudabbir*, absolutely immaculate! Exactly eight months down from the Walmart day, I signed my book contract. Some of the chapters I finished in less than two days. I could not sleep because all day I would be drafting sentences in my mind, and as soon as the kids would go to bed, I'd be on my laptop typing furiously; it was just too much to contain within. And while I was writing, sometimes, the ideas would come up for another book, which I would write down in a separate notebook. It may sound easy, but believe me, it wasn't. Some days, it was scary as hell. My initial fear was, what if I don't have enough to say? I kept saying this to my editor. I didn't want a measly handbook that no one would take seriously. Some days, the ideas in my head would come out all wrong on paper. I had to write and rewrite until it made sense. Some days, all my ideas looked so rubbish that it made me anxious. What if no one wants to read my book? What have I gotten myself into! Panic, panic, and panic! There were times when I changed the full structure of the book. I didn't know the end, but I kept going on, because with all the fears and uncertainty, my adrenaline wasn't going anywhere; it was there to stay, inside of me, and drive me crazy if I didn't do anything about it. If I'd reach a dead end, I'd twist and turn until I found my way through it. Because, my friend, there are no full stops in the passion ride, just commas to test if you are still interested. After all, it was my legacy and no one else's. I remember back in 2012 when I edited our Graduation Edition Magazine, I wrote in the Editor's note:

> **The purpose of this magazine is to share our individual trials with the hope that it may give strength to the people who follow later on and to serve as a reminder for ourselves to go further and beyond.**
>
> يَا أَيُّهَا الْإِنسَانُ إِنَّكَ كَادِحٌ إِلَىٰ رَبِّكَ كَدْحًا فَمُلَاقِيهِ — الإنشقاق- الآية 6
>
> *O mankind, surely you must strive (to attain) to your Lord, a hard striving until you meet Him.*

I realised that eight years back I had pretty much written the purpose of this book and the reason for becoming a Life Coach: to inspire others, and to grow alongside in the process. I realised that the struggle has never stopped since then. I have just not been able to identify it.

The same was the case when I wanted to run the 10k road race a few months after my ankle surgery. I practised fast, I practised slow, I limped, I iced, but since it was fed in my system, there was no way but to just get done with it!

You may say I am selectively passionate, but when I am, I am blinded. I don't know how I would get to the end; all I know is there is no way around it. Then there is no day and no night for me; either I am working on it or planning about it.

Why am I telling you about it?

Because Angela Duckworth, a relatively new psychologist, founded the Grit theory, a study looking into **why some people are successful and others fail.** Her TED Talks has more than 200,000 viewers, and her theory has been taken up by a storm.

Duckworth discovered that success isn't determined by the capacity to learn quickly, good luck, social intelligence, IQ scores, and physical health. Instead, Duckworth summarised that high achievers are people who have a passion, perseverance for learning, and a willingness to overcome failure. According to her, being aware that you are the person who controls your motivation and outcomes is, in fact, what drives success.

I don't want to go into a lot of detail about her research, but I would most definitely want you to go ahead and read her book; it has become one of my favourites while researching for my own. What I want is to take up her points on how we can check where we land on the grit-graph and to apply it to our subject matter of *hijab* and general achievements in the way to becoming a successful *Muslimah*.

1. Courage:

It is a principle of *tafsir* to understand a matter by its opposite. For example, light is understood by its counterpart, i.e., darkness; good is understood in contrast to bad. Allah created opposites so we understand the value of each of them better. And this is the principle used abundantly in Quran to explain concepts.

The opposite of courage is fear. It is natural to fear something when you try something new—the fear that you feel when you try wearing the *hijab* for the first time, for example. But the test of grit is will you go through with it regardless of the fear?

Courage is needed at two levels. First, to start the journey, and then to not stop when trouble comes. The essence of grit is not to give up. You will hear all kinds of voices around you when you embark on the journey to your goal. You will second-guess yourself. You will be discouraged. It's all-natural to feel the fear, but don't let it overpower you.

Duckworth explains as follows:

> **My father would literally say things like "You're no genius," to me… But he would also say things to my mother, who was an amateur painter, like "You're no Picasso." He would say to my sister and me, "You're never going to win a beauty pageant."**

What made her successful eventually was what she calls the "underdog mentality." She says,

> **"I don't think it was conscious, but I've always had the identity of someone who is, you know, 'I'll show you.' These are the words that go through my head when people tell me I can't do something, which is a signature self-talk to the kind of people I study."**

The first step to wearing *hijab* is also courage. You have to take a stand for something you believe in and show it blatantly in your actions. When you are on this journey, maybe the closest people to you don't really agree with you. Maybe because they are close to you, and they really want to save you from being the "odd one out," or maybe because they don't agree with the school of thought you are about to pursue. In any case, the first step is bravery and the courage to stand up to your vision.

Know that it is Allah who holds all the power in this earth, and He esteems bravery. Fear is natural, but to overcome it is extraordinary. To walk out of your comfort zone and remind yourself to have **"eyes on the goal,"** such is the way of the courageous. This is how you get to succeed in this world and the hereafter.

2. **Hard work:**

It is as simple as this: the more work you put into it, the better it will be. Bring to mind the words of your parents and teachers, remind yourself of every time they told you to work harder, and know that they were right. Sometimes there is nothing more boring than hard work and practice. But the truth is that this is the only way to be good at something. There is no skill that comes without hard work. The more you work, the better you get at it, the better you get at it, the easier it gets. **Duckworth believes hard work is more in line with grit, rather than talent, IQ, or any genetic preference.**

Now take *hijab* again as an example. From your efforts in the way of your *imaan* to trying different *hijab* styles until you earn the confidence, it's nothing but hard work. And you must be committed to do it. You may fail sometimes, and you may have the urge to give up, but success lies in getting up and trying again.

Sometimes people give up either because it is difficult or it is taking too long. You might see your friend making better progress in the same thing that is so difficult for you. But research says that you can be equally good if you persistently work hard. The secret ingredient is hard work. Some words are uttered so often that they lose their meaning; you may feel the same about quotes and quotes on hard work. But know that hard work has found its due praise with the fruit it brings.

3. **Endurance:**

Endurance goes hand in hand with hard work. It is to not

giving yourself the permission to give up. You may take a while to sit down and cry, you may take your time to be frustrated, or you may take rest, but giving up is not an option. **"Successful people make a decision fast and change them slow."** It is you developing a thick skin. It is you not letting small failures bring you down.

When you have larger-than-life goals, it takes a while to get there. How do you stay put? You do so by breaking the big goal into smaller, achievable targets. Every time you achieve one target, your confidence boosts, you are excited to achieve more, and you are one step closer to your actual destination. It is important to list your small goals leading up all the way to your ultimate goal. It helps you to look forward to something and look back and gauge how far along you have come.

Buckworth says, **"Small wins are enormously important. We look at people and we say, "Oh, they have this outside confidence," but really, one of the things that builds confidence is actual evidence that you're on the right path."**

When it comes to *hijab, hijab* is not the ultimate goal but a means to an end. It is not religion itself but a part of it. It's a portion or a piece that we need to complete the full picture. Its purpose is ultimately to please Allah. Yes, you may have to take steps to perfect your *hijab*, but you should know that *hijab* itself is a step. When wearing *hijab*, it should not make you think that the job is done but that you are one step closer to your goal.

4. **Resilience and Optimism:**

Resilience is your ability to bounce back after a setback. It's the attitude "all is well that ends well and that which doesn't." Sometimes people are not able to get up after a setback. Resilience is learning from the failures and not being negative about them. Failure too is there to teach you something. Take the lesson and move on. Resilience is knowing the fun is in the game and the learning is in the journey. The learning only comes when you get down on your knees and get your hands dirty. Not every experiment can be a success—speaking of which, I really think scientists are the most resilient of species. They don't give up until they get what they set out to do, like finding a cure to a disease or inventing a new device. Even if they don't know what works, they leave after themselves a theory of what didn't work and make the job easier for the coming generation by ruling out the options. Every big name in history had to go through failure—Steve Jobs, Einstein, and Tesla, among others; anyone doing anything unique had to experiment and had to fail at some point. The point is to not stop there, but to start over. Optimism is the frame of mind that doesn't let you become hopeless.

In matters of *hijab*, maybe you tried many times but never were able to stick through it. Tell yourself it's okay to fail, but not okay to give up. Feed your mind with the affirmation that you will try again and succeed one day. Go back to the times that you have failed and think, what can I do differently to succeed this time? Most of the time, it's a very silly thing that we are not taking notice of which fails us. As my father would say, retract your armies, re-strategise, and attack!

5. **Excellence versus Perfection:**

We have all grown up trying to be the perfect Muslims. Allah loves "*Ehsaan*," we were taught.

But what is *Ehsaan*?

> *The man asked, "O Allah`s Messenger (saws). What is Ehsaan?" The Prophet replied, "Ehsaan is to worship Allah as if you see Him, and if you do not achieve this state of devotion, then (at least, take it for granted that) Allah Sees you."*

When we know Allah is watching us, we can't be any less than the best. And we mortal beings, try to do our absolute best, but being the mortal beings that we are, guess what, we fail too. And when we fail, comes rushing in the guilt and frustration that "we are not good enough," which either send us towards giving up or trying hard but this time with a negative self-image.

Where did we go wrong?

We were not able to distinguish between perfection and excellence. These words look similar but suggest something worlds apart.

We humans are "not perfect," and we cannot create "perfection" even if we die trying. Perfection is the Attribute of Allah. He is perfect, in all His Beauty, His Grandeur, His plans, and His executions of those plans.

We are, as they say, cucumbers with anxiety, a body of water with too many needs. How can we ever be close to perfection? What *Ehsaan* actually means is "to do our best," and "to give it our best shot!" Even that is too hard for people like me. I am never good enough for myself, let alone for a task Allah ordained on me. So how do we go about it?

This concept was best taught to me by Sheikh Mohammad al Shareef who says:

> *"Ehsaan is not perfection, it's excellence. Strive your best, but tolerate mistakes as well. Only Allah (سُبْحَانَهُ وَتَعَالَى) is perfect. Don't be like the shopkeeper who keeps the door to his shop closed all the time in order to keep it clean. No customers enter. If you're always closed and looking for perfection, you'll shut down. When in doubt, kick-start your project as 'Version 1.0' and build on it."*

Excellence is trying hard. Not sitting by the spilt milk is part of excellence too.

Again, in terms of *hijab*, you may let a bit of your hair show, or you may show a bit of your wrists, but don't kill yourself over it. Don't stop covering up completely just because you can't do it perfectly. But on the other hand, don't settle either. The criterion is to get up and try each day. The excellence is of efforts, and not of deliverance.

> *Prophet said, "By Him in Whose Hand is my life, if you were not to commit sin, Allah would sweep you out of existence and He would replace (you by) those people who would commit sin and seek forgiveness from Allah, and He would have pardoned them." (Sahih Muslim)*

So to summarise, if there is anything you want to achieve in your life, you need to be gritty. You need courage, hard work, endurance, resilience, and excellence. And the good news is, Duckworth thinks **we can learn to be gritty.** But for that, she says "self-awareness" has a role to play because how will you cure a disease if you feel you are not sick.

To tell you the truth, grit is all about showing up. For *hijab* and all the other things that you want to get good at. Try, try, try, and never give up. It's as simple as that.

> Our greatest weakness lies in giving up. The most certain way to succeed is always to try just one more time.
>
> — THOMAS EDISON

7

BURJ KHALIFA OF DREAMS

You can never be happy living someone else's dream. Live your own. And you will for sure know the meaning of happiness.

— Oprah Winfrey

Have you seen those Mission and Vision statements most educational institutes have on their pamphlets/books/receptions?

Our vision is to big-fat-word, big-fat-word, big-fat-word.

Yes, those kinds of words which make them look oh-so-professional and give us the impression that they want to reach for the stars and know how exactly to get there too. Man, I have always been so jealous of people with such clarity. I mean, how are people so focussed? How do they know what exactly do they want? How can they see and plan so far ahead? Whereas I, I trip on the table right in front of me and land on my face too.

I mean, there are so many things I want to do, and I

do too. But sometimes, there is no building in the picture. All my bricks are mostly there on the floor, proudly being their own individual selves and refusing to bind themselves to each other. As far as my mission is concerned, it is to get these moody bricks to get along and for once, build something for me. Even if that is a Lego tower.

My life goes mostly like this: I wanted to learn the Quran. Then I wanted to teach. But wait, I wanted to have more children too. The moment they were out of my body, I wanted to be an artist. Oh, and I've always loved to cook for my family. And hosting is my passion. I love setting up long, elaborate buffet tables. And I've always loved working out… I would die but lift more than the person beside me. And running is my latest addiction. Did I tell you I had a foot injury and that I limp after two minutes straight into running? But I still do love it so. Speaking of working out, I taught yoga for a few years, back in the day. And calligraphy is a skill every artist should learn, so let me do that too. And I love to socialise, but have an introverted side too. So let me give both sides of mine equal time. And book club! I always wanted to be a part of one, and I love my book club buddies! And writing too, so let me start a blog. And travelling, oh, how I love travelling! I wish I could travel the whole world! And photography, there is nothing more sensual than a good picture. And whenever I get a chance in my life, I am finishing that Masters in Literature, which was left hanging after my first child. It is important for me to help people. So let me be a Life Coach too. But then cleaning and maintaining the house is important too; it is my duty as the lady of the house. And the kids need me, each one of them, individually. And the picks and the drops and the playdates. And my husband, who I vowed to give my life to, and the relatives, I will be asked about them in the Hereafter. And then there are my *ibadahs*, prayers, *azkaars*, Quran, and some more. I can't sacrifice my spiritual side, you see.

This is me in a nutshell. And these are my bricks. All too far away from a "Vision" or a "Mission." This is me, being a good Muslim/mom/friend/wife/sister/daughter, but then there are 2.8 billion Muslims who are doing the same, and most of them are much better, high-achieving individuals. Whereas I am a jack of all, trying to fit into each box and failing most of the time.

So yes, when I would look at the Vision and Mission statements of other successful people, it would set me off on a journey of wistfulness. Who are these people? Why are their thoughts so organised? How are they so structured?

I've wanted to achieve so much! So much that I can't sleep at night. My adrenaline is pumping all the time. I want to achieve everything! Everything that this infinite world has to offer.

And so, with all that I would like to achieve, there was something of the utmost importance, something that had to top the list of all that was already in motion. It was to build up all my bricks into Burj Khalifa. The Burj Khalifa of my dreams—sounds just about right.

They say when the student is ready, the mentor shows up. And I wasn't about to settle until I found mine. I took every workshop that was being offered in Dubai, Sheikh Mohammad al Shareef, Spencer Lodge, Natasa Denman, Moustafa Hamwi, Natalia Gomez, Sara Powell, Mariam Halawani, and Dr. Dorris are a few of the names which impacted me the most. In addition, I took numerous online workshops on Instagram presence, sales, Etsy shops—you name it. Whether I applied the knowledge is a different story, but the point is, I was searching vehemently for that one pot of gold. I didn't leave any stones unturned. And guess what, I didn't find one pot, but a pocketful of gems from each of them.

My father often says, "When you watch a movie, any movie, look for that one inspirational quote that sets you in the right direction." And that's what I did. I always kept a small diary in my bag and wrote anything that inspired me even the tiniest bit. And now I have a bunch of diaries full of scribbles that console my heart when things don't make sense.

All the soul-searching and questionnaires led me back to my childhood dreams. What did I want to be when I was a little girl? And this was the result of my furious soul-searching.

I wanted to be a good Muslim.
I wanted to be seen.
I wanted to be an artist.
I wanted to be a teacher.

Awareness is half of the cure. And I was blatantly facing all that I have wanted all along. But this all I had already achieved, or was on the way to it at least. All these were small milestones, but where would this all lead to?

Before leaving for Paris for my Carrousel du Louvre exhibition, when I visited my mum, she was all so happy with my achievements; she said, "I am so happy that you have finally found your purpose of becoming an artist." As happy as I was to hear praise from my mom, I wasn't really comfortable with the picture of me only being an artist. I said, "I wanted to be an artist, but that's not the purpose." "Then what is your purpose?" she said. To which I said, "I don't know yet, but it is not to become an artist."

With years of vision-boarding and pinning the common factors, this is what it boiled down to.

It's big, and it's what keeps me up at night. My Vision and my Mission now is crystal clear. It makes my heart beat like it will jump out of my throat. It is what will take me to my Allah in peace with all the skills and craziness He blessed me with. It is He who did not let me settle for less. It is He who sent me on this path and kept on throwing cues at me at every step.

So here goes my collection of Big Fat Words, My Vision

Statement:

> **I want to empower young Muslim girls to embrace their religious identity and live a fulfilling life by pursuing their passions.**

There. I said it.

I was a very silly girl who once had no direction. It took me a long, long time to realise my mission. Heck, I am thirty-seven! That's how long it took. But I would want you to cut to the confusions. In my quest to find myself, I realised there must be thousands like me who want to achieve everything in this world. Why should they not be pursuing their passions, being the sportswomen, the artists, the speakers, being everything they ever want to be? And that too while being true to our collective and ultimate mission of pleasing our Lord in the end?

Why am I telling all of this to you in a book about *hijab* lifestyle? Because once you cover your head, automatically the aunties of the world and the people around you will expect from you piety of a level that kills all inspirations (notice the sarcasm). Sadly, with all the information in the world, and all the advancements around us, that's how the equation is in the minds of most people:

> **Hijab = Lack of inspiration, aspiration, and will to achieve anything in life.**

Until and unless you want to prove them right, you have to get up and do what I tell you to do.

So here is my breakdown in basic steps:

1. Create a map:

Be the detective. Like those series on Netflix and their intricate maps with the red thread connecting one clue to the other. Don't miss out on any hint. Everything that crosses your mind, or everything you had the slightest wish to be, write it down. From your childhood's silliest dream, to what you admire in a person today. Keep jotting them down. The repetition and intersection will help you boil it down to a few basic ones like I did.

I used to have flashes of visions that I kept on ignoring. I had waking visions of strokes of paints and having an audience while I speak. But I kept on ignoring them. But each vision was a message from my subconscious, which I understand now. Try to understand what your subconscious mind tries to tell you. Don't ignore anything. Write down your dreams too, even if they are too big to scare you. No hint is small. You are destined for higher places; it is high time you get comfortable seeing yourself there. *Hijab* is only step one. It sets you apart from the rest. It reminds you every day what you are in it for. Don't let it go. If you are still not able to wear it yet want it, write that down too.

> Goals in writing are dreams with deadlines.
>
> —Brian Tracy

2. **Vision board is the vision road:**

I cannot emphasise this enough. Vision boards bring your dreams to life. They give you permission to envision where you want to see yourself. I have been making vision boards since my first Visionaire workshop with Sheikh Mohammed Al Shareef (which was a long time back!). I keep Ramadan to sit and envision what I would like to achieve for the rest of the year. It gives me a perspective and helps me set the pace for the rest of the year. After I sort out my innermost desires, I pray for them like crazy. Every year, almost all of my *duas* are accepted, *Alhamdulillah.* Such is the blessing of having learned scholars among us. They teach us how to put things in perspective. I am eternally grateful to him for teaching me how to achieve my dreams.

> One way to keep momentum going is to have constantly greater goals.
>
> —Michael Korda

3. **Dreams and roads:**

You have to differentiate between a long-term goal and a short-term goal. For every Muslim, the ultimate mission is to see the face of his/her Lord, Allah جل جلاله. But we need to decide how to get there. Your vision will be that decision. The warriors go and conquer the world, the scholars bury their heads in books to find their way through, and the *huffadh* engrave the words of Allah in their hearts. So, I ask you today. What will be your way to your destiny? So that when you die, you have a legacy that will speak of your struggles. Which of your contributions to this world do you want to be the witness for you in the end? Give your mind the permission to wander; give yourself the consent to daydream. It is only with that you will find your way. It doesn't have to be just one, it can be as many as you can handle.

> The key to realising a dream is to focus not on success but significance—and then even the small steps and little victories along your path will take on greater meaning.
>
> — Oprah Winfrey

4. **Your Deen is for this world, not the next:**

Every time I got busy with my artistic endeavours or read any non-religious book or practised running for a marathon, there was always guilt in the back of my mind. "I am wasting my time." "I could be using the same time for my religious endeavours." "This is all so worldly, why am I so much in love with the world?" For years, I could not pick up a book except for the Quran. In my mind, it was like committing treason. I was ashamed of charging money for my art workshops and paintings, as the "pieties" are supposedly not concerned with the materials of this world.

Until I walked out of my limiting perspectives, I was not able to perform. If anything, long hours on TikTok should be accountable, not me working on my health, vocabulary, or skill. We have to connect every supposedly worldly endeavour to our ultimate purpose. Remember: We cannot make *haram*, what Allah made *halal* for us. We need to stop putting limits on ourselves in the name of religion. Khadija رضي الله عنها was a successful businesswoman; she couldn't have done so without asking for money, and she was more pious than all of us put together. There were warrior women who fought alongside men in the times of the Prophet ﷺ like Hind رضي الله عنها. How was she supposed to do it without leaving the house at all? Let me tell you how: by being within the boundaries of Shariah and not killing their drive that Allah had installed in them. Killing your inner ability is not why Allah placed it so. It is there to be channelised and to work through it towards the plains of *Jannah*.

Everything is a means to an end. Khadija رضي الله عنها bought *Jannah* with the money she earned by helping her husband in her mission. Money was not her goal, but it was the means to reach her goal. Allah has not put any limits on us as long as what we do is within the boundaries of rules slated by the *Quran* and *Sunnah*. Every woman is created differently. We are not clones. Islam is for everyone; it is as much for the housewives as for the working women. I know many women who are walking out of their homes as a single bread-earner for their children, having no *mehram* to support them. In the process of idealising the stay-at-home mums, we have forgotten those who have no other choice.

And to be honest, every woman of our *ummah* should be prepared for the worst, with some kind of skill, education, and experience. Staying at home and raising good kids is ideal, but what if we are not given that choice?

Recently, I needed to have a sports surgery done, and there was not even one female ortho surgeon available, and I had no option but to go for a male surgeon. We have many capable lady doctors *Alhamdulillah,* and they are balancing their jobs at the expense of their families, but there is still a gap in the society where women are needed. At least a few of us should have the vision to go the extra mile. Because, why not? When I look at the research works of NASA, it boggles me what a human can achieve. It is slightly off-topic, but it makes me marvel at the ability of the human mind. We women are gifted with the amazing ability of compassion. How are we utilising it alongside the many abilities Allah has encoded us with? There are many women doing amazing work in every corner of the world: women excelling in fields of helping people with disabilities, and some soaring high on the tech field or the economic front. It fills me up with pride to see women serving their higher purpose. If you feel you are needed at home to raise your children, do so with pride, but alongside help another woman reach for her dreams, be it your daughter or your sister. Volunteer to babysit for her kids; provide her with home-cooked food. Because there are fields where women are needed, and we have a role to play. There are certain things for which at least some of us have to step up. If we all sit and pray in the comforts of our homes, who will do the hard work? What is our contribution? Being a good Muslim is important, but contributing to the wellness of the society is equally important. What are we doing about that? The first three doctors to give their lives in the way of COVID-19 in Britain were all Muslims. Raffia Arshad became the first *hijab*-wearing judge, and Ibtehaj Muhammad the first American woman to wear a *hijab* in the

Olympics. Such news fills us with pride; shouldn't we be on the first-lines in our respective fields, or at least help those who are doing it? I remember when I was studying, on the way back home, I would always drop by at a friend's place where I knew I was always welcomed, and where I would always get freshly cooked food. I can never forget her favour of feeding me when I would be starving and had no time to cook. If you can't go out, be that someone who feeds others without judgement. Allah loves *Muhsineen*. A *Muhsin* can be a helper too. Find your strength and do what you have to do.

> My goal in life became about accumulating wealth for myself in order to give it away. I had to increase my talents and capacity to achieve greater dreams and goals.
>
> — DAVID KHALIL

5. **Avoid distractions:**

The pandemic of these times is not corona; to me, it is Tik-Tok. As if YouTube was not enough, this is another level of time-waster. Know that every minute we lose in mindless scrolling is a minute away from our goal. I don't mean to scare you, but there has to be a certain level of accountability if we want to reach somewhere in our life. So much of our time goes in mindless scrolling on Facebook, Instagram, Snapchat, and the likes. We all are using it, but we really need to hold ourselves liable for the time we spend on social media. This is the Pacman which gobbles up our time without us realising it. I struggle with it too, believe me. My Pacman is Instagram. I love pictures, and often before I know it, I have spent half an hour of useless scrolling and have achieved nothing. Sometimes at the expense of the time that I could have spent with my children or resting or actually doing some real work!

Useless socialising is also the biggest time-waster. It is most important to spend time with the people you love or with whom you have a great time. But the trend of thoughtless socialising is what will hinder us from achieving our goal. After all, we only have twenty-four hours. We can't be everywhere. If you feel it is worth it, then go for it. But remember, you saying yes to something is saying no to something else. Ask yourself, what I could be doing instead? Is it worth the time, effort, and energy?

Another way you can avoid time-gobblers is by committing yourself to beneficial endeavours. Once you are committed, you have no choice but to focus on the task. Commit yourself to any course, gym routine, or class which keeps you guarded on the way to your goal. When at home, keep the phone away for a certain time of the day, and focus on the task at hand. I leave it in the drawer when in my room or purposefully leave it in my room when working in the kitchen, because I pick up the phone for one thing and a thousand notifications take over me, and before I know it, I am checking out Huda beauty's latest makeup tutorial.

6.   Give yourself a deadline:

Open-ended plans generally dissolve into nothing. You need to give yourself a time limit. Say to yourself, "I will finish this project by this time." As bad as I am with deadlines, I thought I could never abide by them. I struggle so much with it professionally. If the client doesn't give me a timeline, I am on for a stroll. Especially with projects in which I know I have to rack my brains. A difficult project automatically sends me into avoidance mode. Everything seems important rather than the task at hand. I'll be mopping the floor like it has been ordained on me by Sheikh Khalifa; my mind will throw useless tasks at me, and I'll happily play catch with them. But we have to hold ourselves accountable if we want anything achieved. Devise a plan that works for you. Tweak it where you feel is the need, but then stick to it like your life depends on it.

> Deadlines just aren't real to me until I'm staring one in the face.
>
> — Rick Riordan, The Lightning Thief

7. Realistic Goals:

When I turned thirty-six, and the panic of being in my "late-thirties" struck, I devised a perfect day-to-day goal plan and held myself accountable by writing about it on my blog. It lasted for a few weeks before I started to stall. Do you know the reason why? My expectation from myself was too unrealistic. One child got sick or one extra errand, and I was thrown off the track. So, I changed it into weekly goals. I gave myself weekly deadlines and a few free days, so that if I lagged behind I had time to catch up. Remember, you can change the plan, but not the goal.

First of all, give yourself achievable goals, and then further divide them into smaller goals. I used to give myself such big goals that a few failures would throw me off completely. Give yourself a treat every time you achieve a goal. That will keep you motivated, and you will feel appreciated. My reward for myself is mostly homemade poached eggs with avocado on a whole-wheat bagel. It's nothing extraordinary, but the thought of having this particular special breakfast makes me happy every single time.

> A goal that's a year out is a very far away dream, and so it's helpful to break those goals down into smaller pieces.
>
> — Rachel Rofe

8. **Treat yourself right:**

I am the biggest punching bag for myself. Every mistake, every delay, or every unaccomplished mission—guess who is the culprit: Me! Of course, it's me! It's my journey and no one else's. But sometimes, we need to cut ourselves some slack too. It's okay to make mistakes; they teach us what not to do the next time. It's okay to take a nap at odd times if your body demands it. It's okay to go out for a leisure walk if that's what will set you right. It's okay if you want to be home alone, not wanting to meet anyone, and it's equally okay to go out and have a good time with your friends.

> You are in a much better position to serve others when your basic needs are met and your "tank is full."
>
> — MICHAEL HYATT

9. **Take help when you need it:**

Delegate work if you have to, but make time for things that are important to you. You are no superwoman; take help where you need it! Hire a cleaner, a trainer, a Life Coach, or ask a friend to help you. Give your clothes to the laundry if you have to. There is no extra merit for doing everything yourself. Help the economy, and take the help! Don't burn yourself out on tasks that others can easily do for you. And if you need help, cry out for help! People are no mind readers; they won't know if you don't tell them that you need help.

Guys what I mean is, don't treat your *hijab* as a shroud. You are not dead; you are more alive than ever before. *Hijab* is step one, and the sky is the limit. Imagine yourself in all the crazy places you want to be—on top of the mountain, or under the water with colourful sea creatures around you; fill up your bucket list, devise your plan to get there, and then show up when it's time.

I still have a long way to go with my Mission and Vision statement, and many of those blocks are still on the floor. But the good news is, I am making progress every day, or at least every other day. The bricks on the floor serve as my stepping stones, while a more aware me, skip my way up to the *Burj* of my dreams.

> When I'm old and dying, I plan to look back on my life and say, "Wow, that was an adventure," not, "Wow, I sure felt safe."
>
> — Tom Preston-Werner

8

BE A MOUTHFUL

*Let people feel the weight of who you are, and
let them deal with it.*

—John Eldrege

I am a fast eater. I love mouthfuls. I love the feeling of food touching all sides of my mouth. The small bites just don't make sense; it's like your tongue is on a search. "Where did that tiny one go?" No matter what *eid-milan* the food is having in your mouth and how much you're enjoying it, the fact is, mouthfuls are not pretty to look at. Small bites are, on the other hand, more poised and controlled. And everyone wants to look at something that doesn't make them uncomfortable. Now I am anything but conventionally poised. The *abaya* may fool you but not for long. Once you get to know me, the mouthful persona pushes in with full force.

I took the most time writing this chapter, because in order to write this, I had to go back to the times when I was, in fact, reduced to a bite-size. People are what they are, but they can be made a better or worse version of themselves. And sometimes, it happens as a response to the impact of our society. It is the small words whispered in our ears, "You are brilliant," or "You are not good enough," which cause the ripple effect. We tend to wear people's opinions and mirror their expectations. What we sometimes fail to understand is that every person is unique. Whatever bad we may think is there, it can be managed, and it doesn't have to be internalised.

I am generally the go-getter, hard-working kind, and my resilience has always worked in my favour. I don't give up easily. But a few years back, a series of events threw me off real bad. It was indeed the plan of Allah that from almost everywhere I got to hear the whispers like, "You are not good enough." It was in such repetition that I had no choice but to accept it. I questioned my credibility in all areas of my being and came to the conclusion that I was, in fact, not good enough for anything. I stopped writing on my blog almost completely and suffered from a writer's block, which lasted for years. I was scared to share my opinions. I was scared to upset people. I was scared to be myself.

When you doubt yourself, the first thing that gets deleted from your life is your vision. The darkness that envelops you ensures you that your fate is to sit alone and lament the shortcomings that you have. It takes away the drive to do better, and to be better. It slowly takes away the pleasure from everything that you enjoy in your life, replacing it with self-doubt. And self-doubt it was, growing thicker by the minute. Until one day, I was sitting at my teacher's office in ATIC Psychological and Counselling Centre bawling my eyes out. I wouldn't say it was the day everything changed, but it was definitely the day when the ball started rolling to the other side.

She spoke a few words, but in those few words, she reminded me of the best things in me. Later, she handed me a printout which said,

Our deepest fear is not that we are inadequate. Our deepest fear is that we are POWERFUL BEYOND MEASURE. It is our light, not our darkness, that most frightens us. We ask ourselves, who am I to be brilliant, gorgeous, talented, fabulous? Actually, who are you not to be? You are a child of God. YOUR PLAYING SMALL DOESN'T SERVE THE WORLD. There is nothing enlightened about shrinking so that other people won't feel insecure around you. We are all meant to shine, as children do. We are born to make, manifest the glory of God that is within us. It's not in just some of us; it's in everyone. And as we let our own LIGHT SHINE, we unconsciously give other people permission to do the same. As we are liberated from our own fear, our presence automatically LIBERATES OTHERS. (MARIANNE WILLIAMSON)

Here is the picture of the actual printout:

> **OUR DEEPEST FEAR** is not that we are inadequate. Our deepest fear is that we are *POWERFUL BEYOND MEASURE*. It is our light, not our darkness that most frightens us. We ask ourselves, Who am I to be brilliant, gorgeous, talented, fabulous? Actually, who are you not to be? You are a child of God. *YOUR PLAYING SMALL DOES NOT SERVE THE WORLD.* There is nothing enlightened about shrinking so that other people won't feel insecure around you. We are all meant to shine, as children do. We were born to make manifest the glory of God that is within us. It's not just in some of us; it's in everyone. And as we let our own *LIGHT SHINE*, we unconsciously give other people permission to do the same. As we are liberated from our own fear, our presence automatically *LIBERATES OTHERS*.
>
> MARIANNE WILLIAMSON
>
> WWW.LARACASEY.COM

I did not believe anything that piece of paper said, but I was relieved to know that someone else did. I don't remember how I got where I am today. While I was curled up in my misery, it was as if God carried me and placed me where I was supposed to be and said, "Here, make it work now!" And only from His *taufeeq* I could get up and start walking with wobbly legs, until I was running with full speed.

That part of me still aches; I feel I didn't deserve it, but it taught me lessons I couldn't learn any other way. It was the pulling of the catapult which launched me into the air, and when I opened my eyes, I was flying.

I still have the pulled-down moments in my life here and there, everyone does, but now I have learnt to combat it. I'll mention my tips of the trade here because I don't ever want anyone to feel how I felt. And in your journey of *hijab*, and your quest to find your dreams, you will hear the whisper in your ears making you firm on the belief that "you are not good enough." It will break you into a thousand pieces, but that is not the purpose of those words. They are there to test your strength. To see, are you made up of what it takes? The *shaitan* will play his game of *waswaas* with a full swing, but you have to be a better batsman and say, "Not this time!" and hit it hard with full force. And every batsman needs practice. Loads of it.

When you decide to take your life on a different tangent, know that these whispers will be frequent. You are evolving, and it doesn't come without discomfort. Your *hijab* journey, for one, will be full of these whispers. You have to rise above, take your stance, and be the mouthful even if people around you are uncomfortable with the idea. Self-love it is called. To be comfortable in your skin, and not sacrifice your well-being for the opinions of others. The thing about self-love is, you need it the most when you are at your worst—when you feel you don't deserve to be loved. Like I said, life does throw you in corners where it is just you; it's then that you have to show some faith in yourself, and the compassion that you so often offer to others.

Here are my two cents, from the little that life has taught me:

1. Complete and full reliance on Allah:

One thing that I have learnt is, as flawed as we are, so are the people around us. They will fail us in ways we can never imagine. If you have any reliance on any person, know that he/she will disappoint you in the worst way possible. There is only one being who would never let you down, one being who is and will be your true friend, Allah *rafeequl aala*, the most Sublime companion. In theory, I knew this all along, but till the time I was alone, I didn't actually feel the friendship. And once you have the taste of that friendship, nothing comes close enough. There is a reason we are gifted with loneliness and discomfort: to get in touch with our ultimate potential, and to get in touch with empathy.

Faith is the rescuer in the end, to know that it's not the end, to know in your gut that He has a plan, and the plan is to not to leave you alone crying. There is a door right in front of you that you have to get up and open, but for that, you have to get up and open it. Know there are big things waiting for you on the other side; you just have to rise up to what you are created for. And that will become evident with time. The clue is, never to give up on Him, on hope, and on yourself.

The difference between people who haven't suffered and those who have is, those who have touched the ground know how it feels and can tell you how to get up and get walking.

> Let it rain on some days, let yourself shiver on
> some cold nights,
> So when it's Spring you'll know why it was all
> worth going through.
>
> — SANHITA BARUAH

2. Own yourself:

Sit down with a coffee one day and write all the good and bad things about yourself. The way Allah has created you. See yourself from your own eyes, not how your mum sees you, or your friends, or your boss. How you see Allah has created you in His image. Write the good, bad, and the ugly. And own yourself with all the flaws. Allah made you with those flaws; you were never meant to be without them. He is Perfect, but we are not. The thing to do is try to be the best version of yourself and shine.

Around the time when I was feeling the worst about myself, I went to this Emotional Intelligence workshop where I was asked to write three things that I love about myself. I sat there crying, unable to write even one. Did I not have even one quality? I did, Allah did not create me devoid of goodness. But I was feeling so low that I was unable to see it. This is the kind of ungratefulness that we should never allow ourselves. And I would not allow you too. You are bigger than your doubts and guilt. You have to capitalise on the blessings He has bestowed on you; but before you do that, you have to know what those are. Make a list of what you have achieved so far. It was all you. Own it.

Many interviews later, I still flinch at the part where I have to introduce myself. I may yap about myself all day when I am with my friends, but never when it really counts. I remember once someone was introducing me and was praising my work, and all I did was sit there smiling uncomfortably, till the lady said, "Back me up here, will you? It sounds like I am making this all up!" I am still working on it. I still struggle with managing praise.

We feel it's not humility if we speak of what we have achieved, but it can also go to the other extreme where we deny all that Allah has made us to achieve. We have to strike a balance. We should be able to talk about ourselves without putting ourselves down. We should be able to say "thank you" and take the compliment. It wasn't luck that you landed where you are. It was God's plan and your hard work. When you practice it, you might come across as boastful; if you ever feel that, tone yourself down a bit, but never give it up completely. Strike a balance. You owe it to yourself and to God. Own your faults and mistakes, but the good parts too; then try to minimise the negative and maximise the positives.

> Never complain, never explain. Resist the
> temptation to defend yourself or make excuses.
>
> —Brian Tracey

3. **Have the audacity to grow:**

Growth is scary; it is out of control. We don't know what we'll become; hence sometimes we prefer being complacent. But growth is absolute, or you'll disintegrate. It might mean changing your life patterns; it might mean a change of surroundings; it might mean a completely different you; but this is something you have to do. There will be people telling you that you have changed, and maybe you have, for the better. Your growth might make others uncomfortable; it's uncomfortable for you too. But that should by no means mean that you abort the mission. You pacify everyone, be nice, and carry on.

When Prophet ﷺ was bringing about the change. Can you imagine how many people must have come to tell him he has changed? He was on a mission. He spoke to people, tried to make them understand and when they couldn't, he still got on his way. You are on a mission too; you have to be the best version of yourself and leave a legacy in this world. There is no other world coming where you can do this. This IS for the other world. This is your only chance. Have the audacity to walk out in that *hijab*, even if your friends are uncomfortable, and even if you feel nervous; it is the first step to your new self. Don't give up just now. Think of the butterfly coming out of the cocoon. If it didn't, it wouldn't be a butterfly; it would be a boring old lifeless larva hanging on a branch. You owe yourself to walk out of that larva; the flight will come.

> We can't become what we need to be by remaining what we are.
>
> —OPRAH WINFREY

4. **Find your tribe:**

Your tribe is the people (a) who understand your growth mindset, (b) who are on the same or similar journey as you, and (c) who have been there and know all about what happens next. They may and may not be your current friend group, which doesn't necessarily mean that there is something wrong with your friends. It just means that you are on a different wavelength on this particular matter. We can have many friends and connect to all of them differently. But know that on this journey of self-exploration you will need all the help that you can get. It can be in the form of technical help, ideas, or just moral support. You need a group of people cheering for you, because God knows we all need the cheerers, especially when you are aiming high and doubting yourself. You need someone to smack you on your head and get you to see straight. Look for the cheerers around you; look for the prompt replies to your vulnerable texts. No one wants to come across as vulnerable, but if you have gathered up the courage to share your worst moments or your greatest fears, notice who answered with the most concern. That one is a keeper.

This book was a roller coaster for me, plus I was writing it during the COVID-19 pandemic, so there was a lot of emotion. Every few weeks, I needed a pump, and that pump I got from three different continents. The friends I hadn't spoken to for years became my biggest allies in this project. And then there were my teachers and coaches, whom I'd mostly leave messages which ended in question marks. And then there were authors who were on the same journey as me.

In your *hijab* journey, you will need girls around you who have the same value system; they may be struggling with *hijab*, or they may have already conquered that bit and can help you with what to expect next. You will also need those who respect you and support you regardless of the fact that they wear the *hijab* or not. You should be able to talk about your fears without having to worry about being judged or misunderstood. You should be able to talk about your struggles and deserve to be heard. If your current tribe isn't providing you with this support, it's time to fish for a new tribe. It's not too hard. As Fred Rodger quotes from his mother,

> **Look for the helpers, you will always find people who are helping.**

5. Don't reduce yourself to a "bite-size":

You may have a lot of people around you, and everyone is entitled to their own opinions. There are some who will agree with you and some who might not. Some will even try to convince you that your dreams are actually deluded, and that you will end up in a ditch. Learn to have a thick skin.

When I started wearing *hijab*, I heard a lecture by Noman Ali Khan. It wasn't even about *hijab*; it was about uncles who get under your skins with their overtly personal questions, and if you answer back, they say, "Oh, so this is your Islam?" The advice he gave was, "Don't let anyone get under your skin." It was simple. And it worked. It was the best advice I got, which became my inner voice. "I won't let them get under my skin!" I was called names, and made fun of, but it was like I was given a super power—everything would just bounce off me. It was just wonderful. I was nice to everyone but did my own thing. What I achieved in that span of time, I haven't for the longest of time.

The tip is: Don't stop to argue or defend your cause or to explain your dreams; if they set out to misunderstand you, nothing that you say will change it. Not everyone will love us. The earlier we understand this, the better. It does get lonely, but then Allah sends another tribe along, which lets you tag along. And you go on. You have to rise up to your potential; you have to be big in what you do, and anyone rolling their eyes behind you should not rob you of it. Your life choices should not be overshadowed by what others think.

> "…and when they pass near ill speech, they pass by with dignity." (Al Quran 25:72)

I often think when Medinah was becoming an Islamic state, how many strong leaders were being born. So many commanders and flag bearers are mentioned; so many warriors and scholars are mentioned. Each one of them a mouthful, and each one of them too big to gulp down. Each of them dedicated to his own purpose; each one of them doing their own thing. Each one of them brought their best to the table, each one of them inspiring in their own right. A loner like Abu Dharr and a larger-than-life leader like Umar were both given glad tidings of *Jannah*, both doing what suited their persona. Their being big didn't make others smaller; it just set the trend for not settling for anything less than their best.

And this, my friend, is what is asked of you. Be a mouthful in all that you do, and do so with grace, empathy, and love. The moments that you were down should serve as a ray of light as to why you should lend a hand to others, but your purpose shouldn't let you sit there. Your uniqueness should pave your way, and your faith should walk you down that path. This is how you will achieve greatness.

> **Do not allow people to dim your shine because they are blinded. Tell them to put on some sunglasses, 'cause we were born this way!**
>
> — Lady Gaga

9

GRACE

A lady laced with grace...
Such, is impossible to despise.

— Ufuoma Apoki

I like comical, I like clumsy, I like big laughter and carefree attitude, and I like wit and originality. I like ease, I like mischievous, and I love the glitter in the eyes right before a great comeback. Heck, I adore all these things in a person. These are what make a person real. This is what I look for in a friend; in fact, this is what I looked for in a husband, and this is exactly what I love about my kids. Ease—that's the crux of it, anything that doesn't comes across as being stiff or uncomfortable. I hate uncomfortable, hate to feel it, or to make others feel it—especially because I am a quiet person, and I have to suffer through it many times. Having said that, one thing that I absolutely admire is grace. You can be all of the above and still have badass grace.

In the previous chapter, I spoke passionately about being yourself and refusing to make yourself small. You would think this aunty is completely off, talking about a mouthful in one sentence and about grace in another. But hear me out; all that you are should be unapologetically you; it should ooze of your individuality, but the grace should be as much part of you as your authenticity is.

What is grace, you would ask, to which I found this beautiful quote by Edmund Burke, which says,

> **Gracefulness is an idea not very different from beauty; it consists of much the same things. Gracefulness is an idea belonging to posture and motion. In both these, to be graceful, it is requisite that there be no appearance of difficulty; there is required a small inflection of the body; and a composure of the parts in such a manner, as not to encumber each other, not to appear divided by sharp and sudden angles. In this ease, this roundness, this delicacy of attitude and motion, it is that all the magic of grace consists, and what is called its je ne sais quoi; as will be obvious to any observer, who considers attentively the Venus de Medicis, the Antinous, or any statue generally allowed to be graceful in a high degree.**

When the matter of *hijab* is in question, I feel grace has to be introduced. You see, you are wearing an *ayaah* of the Quran; modesty and grace have to accompany it. And to me, grace does not mean walking like a swan or a ballerina; grace should generally be a part of your being, almost effortlessly. In your attitude, in your mannerisms, in your language, and in your overall persona. It is that when someone looks at you, they see the family that raised you and the reflection of your religious values. You can be witty and larger-than-life, and still be graceful. You can be a sportswoman, or a comedian—be smashingly good at what you do—and still be graceful. Some people have it naturally; others have to learn it. To be honest, I find myself rough around the edges many times, but one has to keep on trying. It is nothing that can't be learnt.

I read a poem in my college days, which has been a favourite ever since. When I wore the *abaya* the very first time, I felt it kind of spoke about the women of *hijab*; it made me love both of them even more—the poem and my newly acquired attire.

The poem goes like this:

She Walks in Beauty

> She walks in beauty, like the night
> Of cloudless climes and starry skies;
> And all that's best of dark and bright
> Meet in her aspect and her eyes:
> Thus mellowed to that tender light
> Which heaven to gaudy day denies.
>
> One shade the more, one ray the less,
> Had half impaired the nameless grace
> Which waves in every raven tress,
> Or softly lightens o'er her face;
> Where thoughts serenely sweet express,
> How pure, how dear their dwelling-place.
>
> And on that cheek, and o'er that brow,
> So soft, so calm, yet eloquent,
> The smiles that win, the tints that glow,
> But tell of days in goodness spent,
> A mind at peace with all below,
> A heart whose love is innocent!

Lord Byron (excuse his credentials here) wrote this about his cousin, Anne Wilmot, who was a young widow in a mourning dress. Ever since I read this poem, I never got over it. What grace would that be, that with a broken heart and grief, she carried it so well that her description has carried over for over two hundred years. They say the poem speaks of her inner strength more than her outward beauty. Carrying grief with grace—that's really something.

Here are a few areas I feel it is absolutely essential to have grace in, without which you might be wearing the *hijab* but missing the essence of it. Here are little tips on how we can try to be more graceful:

1. **Mannerisms:**

Good manners are a winner in any culture. And they give you away in minutes. Simple things that your mum is always shouting at you for, like, "Sit with your legs folded," or "Eat with your mouth closed"; they really are a thing. Watch your manners, ladies; they really go a long way. As a kid, I was always shy to say *salaam*. I always thought my shy smile would give me off as a nice girl, but no, ma'am! People held grudges multiple times. I was in trouble countless times because adults thought I was being rude, which really, I wasn't! I was just very, very shy. So, when I became a mum, I forced my kids to say their *salaams* even if they had to choke, and I told them my story multiple times so they know that it can really be taken as an offense.

There is another story that I felt I learnt a lot from. We lived in apartments where the swimming pool had separate timings for ladies. One day, my father-in-law went for swimming but came back fuming. When we asked, he said, there were some ladies who dived right in with their *abayas*. While they might be having a good time, others were not; it was uncomfortable for others to see their *abayas* swelling up on the surface of the water. Should people look? Should people not? It was an unpleasant experience for people around, like my father-in-law. Not only did that give a distasteful impression of the ladies but also of the whole *abaya* community. We all have heard generalisations, and we all have cringed at them. So, in the hope of saving themselves and others from the unease, it would have been better if they would have gone during the ladies' timings, worn a burkini before diving in, or resisted the temptation of having a good time while in *abaya* and having an audience.

By that, please don't think I am discouraging women from any sports activities. I am all for it; rather I am one of the crazies participating in road runs in an *abaya*, but the grace has to be maintained—that's all I am asking.

> **A gentleman is not defined by the content of his wallet or the cut of his suit. He is defined by his manners and the content of his character.**
>
> —Anonymous

2. Cleanliness:

Imagine someone absolutely stunning just entered the room; she is dressed like a dream, she makes her way through the hall as elegantly as anyone could, all eyes are on her, and then she passes by you smelling of onions! You hold your breath like you would in a COVID-infected room. And you keep on doing so until she moves away, and God you wish for her to move away. One minute you were trying your best to take a good look, and next you are running for your life. What changed? As nicely as a lady may be dressed, her fumes can put anyone off. We all have experienced that, especially in *taraweeh* in Ramadan. God forbid you stand next to someone who didn't care to change her clothes just because she thought, "I have to wear *abaya* over it anyway!" All your *khushu* goes out of the window, and you patiently wait for the *salah* to be over.

Please ladies, make an extra effort if you take an outer covering, or wear undershirts, or otherwise! It's basic! Especially when it comes to *abayas* because the thin cloth tends to stink in no time! And try to avoid going in the kitchen like a plague before heading out; in the battle of *masala* stink and expensive perfume, masala wins hands down! You are allowed to forget your shoes, but never forget your deodorant! Deodorant is your ultimate friend, especially if you want to keep your friends.

Another thing which can be a major put-off is dirty hemlines. Don't arrive at an event looking like you have waded all the way to get there. The hems of *abayas* or long dresses become dirty very quickly, and it gives a very unkempt look when it does. Make sure you take care of that when in a dusty area, or a muddy area, or when around your kid brother's vomit.

And the breath, oh that bad breath which takes your mind away from anything that you should be thinking, only trying to survive like you would be drowning in a pool, a pool smelling of stale breath. Keep mints, guys! Or cardamom or *paan masala*—anything to save people of that misery.

Apart from that, clean and manicured hands and feet speak a lot about a woman; nobody likes to shake the scaly hands of Medusa.

Keep yourself clean!

> Neatness and cleanliness is not a function of how rich or poor you are but that of mentality and principle.
>
> — IKECHUKWU IZUAKOR

3. **Social skills:**

Even if you are a social freak like me, develop basic social etiquette. Never forget the "please" and "thank-yous." Especially to the servers at restaurants who are serving you. A person who is nice to you but not to the waiter is in fact not a good person. Be welcoming to the newcomers; help loners to feel a part of the group. Be kind to the janitor as you would be to the CEO. Try to know the names of every person cleaning the corridors, and greet them always. Be kind to the person at the help desk, bank reception, or delivery guys. God knows how many times these people are maltreated. These are very basic but very important habits, and they speak of us of who we really are as a person. Basic rule here is, treat others the way you want to be treated.

> Good manners reflect something from inside—
> an innate sense of consideration for others and
> respect for self.
>
> — EMILY POST

4. **Language:**

Language reveals so much about us that it isn't even funny. You are in a bus, and only by overhearing the language of the person, you immediately like or dislike him, even if you don't, you unconsciously place him on a social ladder. You silently declare how polished or not that person is. Don't tell me that you don't, it's unavoidable. The science behind words is insane; words reveal so much about a person.

The use of profanity has increased so much over the years; you won't see a message thread on social media without such words strewn around, especially if it's a political or controversial post. And I would really want to address this in regards to the younger generation.

Know that you don't have to use profanity to fit in. Growing up, I realised quickly that apart from one group that might have found it cool or relatable, people do take profanity for what it is! Know that F word is not cool; it may be used as a verb, a noun, and an exclamation mark, but the fact remains that it is profane nevertheless. Don't give in to the social pressure, or the impulse to fit in. There is so much more to you than some filthy words polluting your tongue.

Be funny, and be cool, but don't take up this road. Before you know it, it will become a part of your diction, and you will be saying it without realising what you just said.

> The foolish and wicked practice of profane cursing and swearing is a vice so mean and low that every person of sense and character detests and despises it.
>
> —George Washington

5. **Humour:**

I am a supporter of humour all the way. I think I've said it multiple times already. But humour loses its touch when it becomes nasty or targets people. It may be targeted at a nationality, religious beliefs, facial features, or someone's inability to do something. In any case, it's not cool. There are many things one disagrees on, but to make fun of someone just because you don't agree with them is just pure mean. We should really watch what's making us laugh. Is it at the expense of someone? We all are guilty of doing it sometimes; it may be as harmless as a chuckle when your friend slipped or spilled coffee. You may not mean it and started giggling. Try to stop yourself and apologise immediately. The point is to stay sensitive to other people, to immediately realise our mistake before we become desensitised towards it.

The same goes for mimicking; it is almost regarded as a form of comedy. You do it once, your friends laugh. You do it again, and before you know it, it becomes habitual. I am not proud of it, but I have to sometimes bite my tongue to not do it. I am good at copying others. It works well if I'm in a body combat class, but it is really hard to stop when it comes to copying accents. Let me tell you, anyone else would hardly ever stop you because it is regarded as funny; you have to do it yourself—stop it in the tracks before it becomes a habit.

Another one is sexual humour; I hate sex jokes. It's just vulgar. I've had to excuse myself millions of times from such conversations. It has become so common that even family comedians use them in their gigs, and you are left looking at your palms, not knowing where to look, if to pretend you are enjoying it or not. And it looks super bad when a *hijabi* is doing it. There are protocols for everything, and the protocol for *hijab* is that you define your limits. People might like it or not; your principles are your own and in this case, defined by God.

These are just a few examples of toxic and contagious habits that we pick up without even realising it. Whether you wear a *hijab* or not, these little things make you a better person. You may be a wonderful person, but if you come across as being nasty, that's what people will believe. Humour is a tricky place, because most of the time, it is regarded as harmless, while sometimes, it's just plain bullying. We really need to know the difference.

> In words are seen the state of mind and character and disposition of the speaker.
>
> — PLUTARCH

6. Empathy:

I have never understood empathy better than these words from *To Kill a Mocking Bird*.

> You never really understand a person until you consider things from his point of view, until you climb inside of his skin and walk around in it.
>
> —ATTICUS FINCH

Empathy makes everything graceful. The fact that you are willing to come down on your knees for people you know or not is the most beautiful thing in the world. The fact that you want to help is noble. But empathy is a technical area, and what you might be feeling might not exactly translate into the actions that the other person might require.

As important it is to feel their pain, it is equally important to approach the matter sensitively.

What I understood as a child about empathy from my mum was, if your friend is feeling down, you tell them you know how it feels. You tell them about how you went through something similar and that it all becomes okay in the end.

To my husband, it is jumping up and saying, "How can I help you? How can I fix it for you?"

To my sister, it is saying, "But think of how blessed you are. People have it so much worse than you," so that they feel fortunate and forget about their pain.

All these approaches may be coming from the right place, and might really work for one as a coping mechanism. What I learnt in my training as a Neuro-Linguistic Practitioner is that these methods might not always work when it comes to empathising with others.

When we start talking about our experiences, whatever integral point we are trying to make, people feel they're not being heard. They feel the focus is taken away from their problem. They came to you to share something that's been upsetting them, and here you are yapping about how you were a superwoman who conquered it while they are not able to. They don't want success stories. THEY JUST NEED TO BE HEARD. They want to vent and let it out. Maybe a directional comment here or there, nothing more. It has to be about them. Only about them. They don't need help or to be interrogated. You can't do anything for them because that's not what they might always need. THEY JUST NEED TO BE HEARD. They also don't need to be told how blessed they are; they already know that. No need to make them feel guilty for what they are already feeling bad about. Anyone can have a bad day or feel pulled down by the daily chores. It's not fair to compare them to the people in Syria or the refugees in Bangladesh. Their feelings are as valid as of those people. They don't need a comparison. THEY JUST NEED TO BE HEARD.

The appropriate and graceful response would be on the following lines: "I hear you," "You are doing great," "You are so brave," "Remember the time you overcame that challenge, I admired you so much for it," "You are not alone," "I am here for you," or "You can do this, I have full confidence in you."

Make them feel heard, loved, and secured. That's all they need from you because in the frenzy of the daily rut, they might not be hearing it very often. We all need to have our doses of positivity and to be told that we can do it. If anyone comes to you crying, just tell them they are doing a great job, and if you have a piece of advice, slide it in gracefully wrapped with compliments. And even if no one comes to you, be kind to everyone generally; you don't know who needs it the most.

> Good manners and kindness are always in fashion.
>
> — ANONYMOUS

7. Forgiveness:

People say weird things all the time; people act weird all the time. Jealousy is a real thing, and so is bullying. In your journey of *hijab,* you will come across all kinds of comments. Why do you wear so much makeup when wearing *hijab*? Why do you listen to music when you are a *hijabi*? Or Why don't you...? Even if you don't wear a *hijab*, this conflict is real. People can be really nasty to you. They don't understand your journey or how much progress you have made. Only you know it, and that's precisely why you should ignore them and move forward. You consciously forgive them because they really have no idea what they are saying, because if they were as enlightened as they assume they are, they wouldn't make another person feel so bad about herself. Ignore, forgive, and walk away.

Sometimes you do feel like answering back, but really, what's the best you can get out of it? They won't change their minds or their perspectives about you, and that would only make you sad/upset/angry. Don't look for closure or give explanations. Don't give them so much space in your head. It's not worth it. If anything, it would keep you diverted from more important things in your life.

But do take a sneak peek at the criticism. It might actually serve you well. Is there even one bit of honesty in them? Do you think you can improve? What kind of a person would you become if you do what they said? They might have not said it in the best way possible, but critics are the best teachers. How would you improve if you are not criticised? Don't take criticism to your heart, but do make the best out of it if it is served to you.

> **The weak can never forgive. Forgiveness is the attribute of the strong.**
>
> — MAHATMA GANDHI

10

WHY DID SHE TAKE IT OFF?

> To overcome fear, here's all you have to do: realise the fear is there, and do the action you fear anyway.
>
> —PETER MCWILLIAMS

When I started writing the book, I included the names of some of the most influential *hijabi* influencers to be used as an inspiration. By the time I got to Chapter 10, many of them have taken off the *hijab* after wearing it for decades. I am no one to judge them as I have taken it off myself, not once but twice; but yes, the heart does feel the grief. It's like they decided not to be in your tribe anymore. And even though you try to understand, it still hurts, and you feel betrayed to an extent. But this is the time to remind yourself that only Allah is perfect and no one else; and that anyone can face tribulations in faith, even after following it for many, many years.

The biggest fear when wearing the *hijab* is, "What if I am not strong enough?" or "What if I take it off too?" I would not disregard this fear completely, because it can happen to anyone. After wearing it for more than a decade, I still sometimes wake up from vivid nightmares in which I enter a place and everyone turns to look at me and say, "You took the *hijab* off?" I wake up panting and thinking it really happened, and resort to making *istighfar* and praying that it never happens to me again.

Let me tell you, *hijab* is the best thing that ever happened to me. I can't imagine myself without it ever. It has become my identity, but yes, it does become difficult sometimes. When I visited the United States, there were multiple times that I saw people looking at me with horror in their eyes like, "Oh my God, she is one of those!" And believe me, I am not talking about any far-off village; it was in the heart of the very cosmopolitan cities. Once on the ferry going to Disney World, my husband was having a very friendly chat with a family, but the moment he introduced me as his wife, their expression changed. They quickly finished off the conversation. On the streets of LA, I remember a guy staring at me with such a piercing stare that I started walking faster. He kept on staring till I was out of sight. I gave a smile, but there was no response; it was a very, very angry stare. It gave me chills for a long time afterward. Yes, most people are very polite, some even inquisitive, but the one-off incident is enough to make your knees wobbly. As surprising as it sounds, even in a city as tolerant as Dubai I have faced discrimination. Once my husband's business acquaintance invited us over; it was my first interaction with them. For a good forty-five minutes, his wife couldn't bring herself to talk to me properly; another guest had to play the host until she became comfortable with having me (or my *abaya*) around. Even in my own country, many people treated me differently because of my *hijab*.

The moment you take up the *hijab*, while the *hijabi* community will be out there cheering for you, there will be some who will make you feel like an outcast. Some of them might actually be your closest ones. And they will be enough to throw you off guard.

The *hijab* high can be a great plus. When you wear *hijab*, as much as you struggle with looking presentable, the high of being noticed and standing out is grand. To be intelligent, and to be performing well in the workplace with your faith wrapped on your head is amazing; you might be the only *hijabi* girl in the football team or the only aeronautical engineer. And the relief of not having bad hair days! The *hijab* high is just awesome! But to be honest, at the same time, you will feel invisible. You will not be invited to many places because it is not *"Islamic"* enough to invite you to; the small talks will become more uncomfortable; people don't know how deep you are in it and don't know what really to talk to you about. Your group of friends might even decrease. To a life full of competition, this might be an added disadvantage.

But with so much of insecurity, why do girls still go through with it? You might ask.

It only happens when your faith is so big that it can't be contained within your heart; it struggles to come out in your appearance and your words. You often speak of Allah سُبْحَانَهُ وَتَعَالَىٰ with such adoration that it leaves them uncomfortable, or you talk about *Akhirah* with such conviction that it's almost bizarre. You have this pull, this constant pull, and you feel there is only one way to go, and that is to take up the *hijab*—at least once, to know how it feels. How it feels to be within the protective attire of your *Deen*, to wear your *Deen* on your sleeve, and to be recognised as a Muslim at the first glance.

I have come across four major reasons as to why most women take off the *hijab*:

1. **Islamophobia:**

The Islamophobic narrative seems to be the most prevalent reason for women taking off their *hijab*. The political situation around the world is not a secret. There are countless narrations of women being called out names, being threatened, or actually being attacked for wearing a piece of cloth their religion demands them to. An article in Broadview mentions,

> It took a verbal attack and someone spitting on her on public transit for Hannieh Amiri to question the hijab she had worn for seven years. She was in Grade 9 and wearing a light purple hijab—a headscarf worn by some Muslim women to cover their hair and neck—one day when she boarded the bus after school. A man rang the bell to get off as soon as she entered, mumbling about the Prophet Muhammad ﷺ on the way to the next stop. "F— Muhammad," Amiri recalled the man saying as he spat on her leg while making his way to the door. "My eyes were tearing up, and it was just humiliating," she said. "Everyone was kind of looking at (me) as if they pity (me)."

This is not a one-off event. These events are becoming increasingly popular, and many women report to have been really scared by these events. I remember one of my relatives living in the United Kingdom saying, **"I can't believe I am feeling scared walking in the streets I grew up in."** Many of them feel scared for their children, and in the heightening anxiety around the world, they take refuge in giving up the *hijab* altogether.

I remember before going to the United States, I called my friend who lives there to ask about the situation. She told me specifically not to wear my usual black *abaya*. I still wore it at some places because of the crazy heat, and because nothing is as breathable as the flowy black material we get in

Dubai. But you see, it is different when you are visiting, and it is different when you live there. I can't imagine being in a situation when you have to prove your innocence day in and day out, without even having a chance to speak for yourself. In the bus, at the grocery store, to feel the eyes on you all the time, to have the worst scenarios playing at the back of your mind every time your kids leave for school. It's hard for *hijabi* women everywhere, especially in places which are not densely populated with Muslims.

Though I know there is an ease in the religion in the matter that you may claim something that you don't believe to save your life. But this is an ongoing issue; Muslim women can't all take off the *hijab*, and let their identity be history. But it IS hard living in these times when Muslims are being marginalised mainly because of their faith and the representation of their faith, i.e., the *hijab*.

Sadly, the *hijab* that was supposed to cover the Muslim women is highlighting them in the most tragic manner. And this is the biggest trial of our times. Those who get on with it, I really admire them. To fight the anxiety every day is not a joke, and those who keep on doing it, clearly have either the nerves of steel or amazing *imaan* levels.

2. Being the alien:

On the one hand, *hijabi* women are highlighted in the worst way possible; on the other, they are made completely invisible. In any given workplace, a woman has to face gender bias, and to top it off, if she is a *hijabi*, her chances of making it become a hundred times more difficult. Women with *hijab* have to prove their intellect, their worth, and their abilities many times more than a non-*hijabi*. The corporate sector, hospitals, universities, or sports—a *hijabi* girl has to barge her way in and prove her credibility. Most complain of being overlooked by their teachers or their superiors like they don't exist. They are socially marginalised by their peers and have to battle the loneliness aside from all the hard work they put in. The first impression, which is most commonly of an oppressed girl who knows nothing about this world, hardly ever makes it through to any other version. Most people come in with a set mindset; they hardly ever get persuaded, unless you are either very good or very lucky.

And to top it off, you are forever expected to be defensive of your faith. You have to have a plethora of evidence to defend your faith and your choice of wearing the *hijab*. You have to continuously tell everyone that it's your own choice, even though anyone hardly believes it. You need to be constantly on guard; to be constantly ignored by those around you leads to all kinds of self-esteem issues. It is hardly a surprise that young girls feel it's easy to be without it, because it is. Nobody wants to be an alien; nobody wants to be hushed off in a corner. You really need to have a lot of guts to go through with it. Though surprisingly, the challenge is what drives some of the girls. Just like the feminists wake up to prove their point, and the nationalists rally to affirm their views, these girls wake up to change the narrative. They wear the *hijab* and work twice as hard to prove everyone wrong. It becomes their mission. And some of them succeed too. Like Ibtihaj Mohammed, Linda Sarsour, and Ilhan Omer—these women have consciously changed the narrative for the *hijabi* community. I do feel that the strength comes with the numbers. When you see many girls around you fighting for the same cause, it gives you strength. You rise as a community. But the fight is mostly on an individual level.

Having said that, there is a majority of girls we don't see who are struggling for their faith quietly, and in the fight, they sometimes give up and opt for the easy option.

3. **Family pressure:**

There are two kinds of family pressures.

a. They force a girl to wear *hijab*.

b. They force a girl to take off her *hijab*.

I have read countless recent narrations of girls being beaten up and forced to wear the *hijab* by their families. You would think they were tales of old times, but they are not. At a tender age, they might even give in to the family pressure, but when they grow up either the thought of what life would be outside the *hijab* leads them to a road of curiosity, or they simply start to detest the piece of clothing forced upon them. More often than not, in these cases, girls lead two personalities: one to please their pious parents and the other to please themselves. In the tug-of-war of "you have to do this" and "I don't want to," the actual reason of why it should be done goes out of the window.

In the other scenario, the family actually joins hands with the outside force which is already at work to stifle the little flicker of *imaan* in the girl. They don't support her choice of wearing the *hijab*, and the girl is left on her own, inside and outside of the house. Sometimes, it happens after marriage; the constant nagging about how she is not as pious as she looks or the blackmailing that goes in the name of good Muslims is enough to dishearten anyone. Who wants to be judged all the time?

4. **Lack of Imaan:**

We all are familiar with the fluctuations of *imaan*. One day you are the ideal Muslim, the next you have to really drag yourself to the prayer mat. It's normal. Sometimes girls start wearing *hijab* after *hajj*, *umrah*, listening to a moving lecture, or being in the company of other *hijabi* girls. But then life takes them away from that *imaan* high and into the rut of work, uni, marriage, or children, and *imaan* takes a backseat. Faith has to be constantly fed, you see; if you are not on guard, it will slip away like the sand. And it happens so frequently. After a soulful Ramadan, we all make promises to stick to reading the Quran and praying on time, but as the month passes, it becomes harder and harder to stick to your promises.

Hijab too in the end is a reflection of *imaan*, and more often than not when the *imaan* goes down, so does the will to wear *hijab*. *Hijab* doesn't support your *imaan*; rather your *imaan* supports *hijab*. One may feel like a hypocrite when on the face of it everyone thinks you are a practising Muslim, whereas in reality, your prayers are slipping away one after the other. If it is not taken care of immediately, the *hijab* seems like nothing but a burden that one carries around. And it comes to a point where you think if it doesn't make you feel religious, then what's the purpose of a cloth on your head anyway?

How can we help?

We all understand that it is hard and it is scary; and that it's not an easy thing to do. But for a girl who could do it in the first place, it's heartbreaking to see she can't do it anymore. So if you are struggling with carrying on with the *hijab*, or one of your friends has given up or thinking of giving up, the only thing we can do is try to understand the problem and deal with it accordingly. What do you think could have caused it? Is she up to talking about it or not?

1. It's nothing personal:

As hurt as you may be, it's not only about the *ummah*. Yes, the image of the entire *ummah* takes a hit when a girl with the following of millions shrugs off her identity as a *hijabi*. But as hurt as you may be, it's her decision at the end of the day—the decision that is between her and Allah. To troll her and make her life miserable or to call her *kafir* and all kinds of names will not bring her back. It's her decision, and as much as we disagree, we have to respect it.

If it is someone close to you, I highly advise you to not shun her out or to start sending her posts about *hijab*. If she has done the *hijab*, she knows the rules very well. Clearly, it's something deeper than what seems apparent. It can be any of the reasons stated above, so chances are that any half-hearted forwarded message will not make a difference. And if you leave her out in the cold, either she will feel betrayed, lonely, and friendless, or she'll go towards the other side where people admire her for not wearing the *hijab*. Don't ask her too many questions; maybe she is not ready. Chances are she might be very defensive of her decision. Let her be for a while, and when she is comfortable around you and whenever the discussion comes up, hear her out, and help her accordingly.

Two of my friends stopped wearing *hijab*; both of them had very different reactions to what I had to say. One of them is very close to me. I always asked her directly about her leaving the *hijab*, and we always had very honest discussions about why she couldn't do it. Every time we met, I would ask her when she will wear the *hijab* again, that too because she said she will one day. Once I didn't ask her about it. When it was time for me to leave, she asked me, "Why didn't you ask about my *hijab*? You always used to!" I said, "I didn't want to come across as pushy." To which she said, "You are my only friend who never stops worrying about my *Akhirah*. I would never want you to stop." The other friend, who also planned to wear it once again, and has started again, *mashaAllah*, used to get annoyed if I asked her. So, I stopped asking her, and was there for her nevertheless. You see, people have goodness in them, but everyone reacts differently to the same stimulus. What might work for one doesn't work for others. You just have to figure out your footing. Never stop being there. It counts a lot. Inclusivity is an important part of our *Deen*. If a person is going through an identity crisis, it's really not fair to leave them alone.

2. Help them with modesty:

The thing with leaving the *hijab* is, people mostly don't just leave it; they flip over to the other side. I say "mostly" because some of my friends drew the line and never stopped wearing full sleeves or loose shirts. As for me, I got married right after I left *hijab*; so in the high of being in love and having no one to stop me, I really went to the other side, even though in my mind I always knew I will come back to it. It might seem crazy, but whenever I got a sleeveless shirt stitched, I'd keep the extra cloth in the hope that when I wear the *hijab* I wouldn't have to waste my entire wardrobe. It's crooked, but that's how it is. And I am sure I wasn't the only one. *Imaan* is a tricky thing to have; there might be a flicker in you, but your desires might take you totally in the opposite direction. It's important to have people around you at such times to remind you even if a little bit. Since I was newly married, I was pretty much cut off from my friends. My biggest aim at that time was to impress my husband, his family, and the people who invited us for dinners. It was much later when I had my own space that I thought of coming back.

If you are really close to your friend who left the *hijab* and is drifting to the other side, you could call her out on it. You can say something like, "I didn't say anything about you leaving the *hijab*, but please don't leave modesty altogether." Remind her that it doesn't seem like her. She might listen, or she might not. Your job is to be there for her anyway, and you must tell her that. And please don't send her random modesty quotes. They don't help. In fact, it makes the person feel super-judged.

3. Teach by example:

To teach her by example you have to be around her. You shouldn't seem judgemental at all. Just be around her like usual when she used to wear *hijab*. No need to verbally remind her. Just be there. Pray together. That's really the most important thing. You wearing the *hijab* and being around her doing all the things both of you love is the biggest reminder in itself. Don't cross your limits when it comes to modesty. That also serves as a good reminder. It teaches others to draw limits as well. And watch your expressions; not even the slightest flinch when she is not abiding by what was once your mutual code. Believe me, she is super sensitive and is watching you very closely. Just be there for her, being yourself. I can't emphasise it enough.

I remember when I wasn't wearing *hijab*, my friend during a discussion said, "I don't want my kids to grow up seeing me without my head covered." It hit me; even though she didn't even realise what she had said. She didn't even have kids then. But her vision was enough for me to have a moment of insight. It partly became the reason I wear *hijab* today. Let it be natural. Let it flow out of you, and your friend might just pick it up one day when you expect it the least.

4. Pray for her:

If you are really so concerned for your friend, more than advising her, you should pray for her in the quiet of your own room, where no one else listens but Allah. That would be the ultimate testimony of your friendship that you worry about her even when she doesn't see you. There is nothing more powerful than a heartfelt prayer. If you see her doing wrong, and your heart breaks, go and pray for her. She might have no one worrying about her *Akhirah* like you do; just translate that into a *dua*. You will be surprised at what your *dua* can do.

> At times you may not be able to help those in need except through prayer. Don't underestimate its power.
>
> — MUFTI ISMAEEL MENK

One thing to remember is, everything happens with the *taufeeq* from Allah سُبْحَانَهُ وَتَعَالَىٰ. If we are able to wear it, it's from Him. If not, then it's taken away for a reason, a reason we must try to find and fix. And when our own faith is so fragile, who are we to point fingers at others? We can worry and pray—that's from the goodness of our heart—but to say anything even slightly off can really spoil the *Deen* for others or for us.

But at the same time, one has to remember how big a responsibility *hijab* is. If you are chosen by Allah to do a good deed, the responsibility comes along with it. You cannot separate one from the other. The perceptible part of *Deen* is such; people start seeing you in a certain manner. There is no compulsion in *Deen*, but once you enter, you have to abide by the rules and leaving it might cause others to follow suit. Similar is the case with *hijab*; once you are in it, you are in with the certain protocol, and your leaving it might cause others to follow. Now one may say, "I didn't mean it to happen," but the consequences, the domino effect will happen, and there is no one to blame except for the one who caused it in the first place.

> It's like a domino effect. After all the time of neatly putting the pieces together, one wrong move, one moment of distraction, and all of it comes falling down. The same happens to us. While ignoring all those moments that happened, all the situations when we wanted to do something, make a move and let our

impulses take over, we put them neatly one behind other and now it comes crashing down around us.

— Anna B. Doe

11

BUT WHAT ABOUT LOVE?

> Boundaries are, in simple terms, the
> recognition of personal space.
>
> — ASA DON BROWN

I am a product of fairy tales. I think all girls of my generation are. Cinderella, Snow White, and Ariel, all of them taught us from early childhood that there can be no wrong on the path of love. That love means to give in. We were taught by these silly stories that love is honest, it is true, and there is no doubting the person you love. After the fairy tales came the Sweet Valley world, the charm of Aaron Dallas, and the dark curls of Todd Wilkins; we were as much in love with them as the twins themselves. But no one told us about the boundaries we were supposed to draw when it comes to love, what consent means, or what are the dangers of predators in the skins of potential love in our lives. The times we grew up in, no one spoke of abuse. Blackmail in the name of love was unspoken of. Religion kept the constant stance of all of the above being *haram*. An assertive full stop right there. No other information was given. Parents were strict, and there was no dialogue when it came to sexual information. It was a forbidden territory, which stayed inescapable with the roaring storm of hormones youngsters didn't know what to do with. There were a lot of hush-hush love stories, and mishaps too, but no dialogue.

The youngsters of today are better informed. Most of them don't believe in fairy-tale love. And they are somewhat aware of their rights and privacy. But there are challenges of overexposure via social media. The curiosity is stronger, and the means are plenty. And I feel it is very important to speak to the young Muslim generation about the dangers that lurk around every corner. *Hijab* is great, but every girl needs to have knowledge about what is the worst that can happen, and that it does happen. Since I feel these are the topics not spoken about in an average Muslim household, someone has to say it. Our young girls are our most prized processions, and in order to empower them, I feel they should be talked to like adults. They should know that these things do happen in the world whether you wear *hijab* or not, and I feel they should know how to handle the situation if ever it occurs.

1. **What if it is love?**

First of all, wait till you are done with your studies if you want to ride this particular bandwagon. Love and ambition hardly ever go hand in hand. Plus, any feeling of "love" that you may feel in your teens is probably infatuation. Wait for it to run its course. It's more the "falling in love with the feeling of being in love" than anything else.

Ibn Abbas reported: The Messenger of Allah ﷺ said, **"We do not see for those who love one another anything like marriage."** (Ibn Majah)

You see, Islam has taken a very no-nonsense stance when it comes to protection of the ladies. The door which can slightly take to the mistreatment of a woman is tightly closed. If a guy sees a girl and falls in love, he should marry her! If he wants to get to know her, he has to do so in the presence of a family member and vice versa! There is no way around it. Dating is not an Islamic option, neither is engagement. I don't want to put you off, but I know of so many cases of girls being maltreated by fiancés; and the girl would not say anything because of the fear of what if the engagement breaks? What if everyone blames her? It is better not to go down that road. Get to know the person in a safe environment and get married!

Let me tell you something. I had a love marriage. "Love at first sight" he calls it. We met through our parents and hit it off immediately. Got engaged the next day, and this year it makes us sixteen years strong. *Alhamdulillah!*

Love is great. It makes life so much better, and it does go a long way. But it has to be a thought-out decision bearing the stamp of *Istikhara*. Allah knows what you don't know. He sees behind the pretence. Trust Him on the biggest discussion of your life. If ever a guy shows interest, keep the parents in the loop.

2. What if it's "not" love?

The feeling of being in love messes with our heads. That's true. The hormones cloud the minds, and no matter how many alarm signs are there, a girl is not able to see it. It might sound like a cliché, but it is the truth. You don't know how true someone else's claim of love is. If he is so serious, he will contact your parents. I know dating is the norm, but please keep your parents in the loop. There is no other way. I read so many cases every day of girls being taken advantage of physically or monetarily by the person they claimed to be madly in love with. It is not the tales of old times; these are real scenarios from today's world. The fluttery feeling of being in love seems so real that it's hard to pay attention to the boring bits. When a girl is being treated like a princess, the maltreatment seems like a very remote possibility; but the number of instances of misconduct around the world is alarmingly high, and most of them start with the sweet appeal of true love. What I am asking you is to be aware and keep a good head on your shoulders.

3. **Social media love:**

As much as it is normalised, social media infatuation is a recipe for disaster in most cases. Innocent girls are made to believe false claims of love. It may be fun for some boys, experiments for others, and actual dark business for some of them out there. You don't know who is on the other side of the screen. What is his intention? How can you even know? Do me a favour; keep your social media space as safe as possible. It's never a good idea to give your address or personal details. Never go out to meet your chat friend even if it's a dare from your friend. It's never safe. Not talking to strangers is as valid for grown-ups as for kids.

4. **No pictures, please!**

No matter how close you are to a boy, just friends or engaged, never give reins of your life in someone else's hands. No inappropriate pictures ever, please. Even if he insists, threatens to end the relationship, or even threatens to kill himself, it's not okay.

Many times, girls are forced to feel responsible and are blackmailed into doing things they don't want to. It includes sending pictures of themselves or meeting alone. And because most of the time their parents are not aware, there is no one to bail them out from such fiascos. Sometimes, the parents might even know about the relationship but not the toxic side of it. Keep your parents informed. Don't hide facts from them for the fear of a bit of scolding.

I often speak to my kids about such topics; some friends

are surprised that I have such an open communication with my fifteen-year-old son. To which I say, "I am the mother; if I don't talk about it, then who will?" It is my job to give him a perspective, Islamic and otherwise. I certainly don't want the Internet to give him answers to what he is looking for. If he can't talk to me about these things in good times, what makes you think he will come to me if he lands himself in trouble? It is so important to give direction to the young adults because there is all kinds of information available on the Internet. We don't know what they talk to their friends in school. All the information I ever got on the hush-hush topics, I got it from my friends or the people who weren't supposed to talk to me about them. My parents were too uncomfortable talking about it, almost like these things don't exist. And we kept it like that for everyone's comfort. But it doesn't have to be this way. With such accessible and distorted information around, youngsters need to have an adult perspective on how things work. What's allowed in our religion and what is not. Why is something regarded as wrong? What to do if you do make a mistake? For starters, talk to your parents, or an adult you trust.

Since we are on this topic, there are a few things I want to point out about sexual misconduct.

Hijab, modesty, lowering of the gaze, and the positioning of *mehram/ non-mehram* are all preventive measures that Allah has prescribed for us. But this doesn't mean that no bad can ever happen. We can't predict what the other person is thinking, or what his intention is. To be cautious, smart, and open about this is as important as the *hijab* itself.

1. **Trust the vibe:**

Vibes don't lie. If someone gives you creepy vibes, he probably is a creep. Learn to listen to your gut. There are all kinds of people out there, the good, the bad, and the shady ones.

The problem is, it's hard to figure out who is who. And because a girl is not really sure, she may resort to being polite. There is no polite when it comes to your safety. It's okay to be rude if someone gives off an "off" vibe. The perpetrators are not always outside our homes; they may very well be within the reach—a neighbour, or a relative. Anyone who seems off, avoid him like the plague and tell your family/friends that you don't have the "right feeling" about him, so even if you act out they'd know why. Learn to listen to your gut and act smart.

2. **Inappropriate remarks/touch:**

Please know that Islam doesn't allow a girl to be alone with a *non-mehram* and to keep a decent distance with a *mehram*. All these rules are there for a girl's own protection.

If you are unsure about any remark, play it back in your mind and ask, "Would my friends/my brother say something like this to me? Would it sound appropriate if they do?" Like I said, if you are not comfortable with someone being around, make it known. Even if it's as minor as the creepy vibes. A girl always knows. No need to self-doubt. Just keep the necessary precaution. If you feel they tried to touch you or used suggestive language, talk to the parents. Don't hint. Use the exact words. There is no *hayaa* (modesty) when it comes to protecting yourself. If you can't say it, write a message to your mum. Say the words, convey the message, and let it be known. If you can't say it to your mum, say it to some adult you trust. If you feel something is inappropriate in your work environment, confide in a friend. Make her your shadow if you feel uncomfortable around certain people. Complain to the higher authorities if you have to. Be rude if you have to be. Scream if you have to.

There is no courtesy when it comes to any kind of sexual misconduct.

Hijab or no *hijab*, react in a manner that no one will dare to even think about messing with you.

A teacher of mine told us to practice an emergency scream. We girls are always told to be so proper that if a misfortune arises, we can't find the voice to support us. Learn to scream! You might not need it, but if you ever have to, your scream should be big enough to get attention.

3. **Identify emotional blackmail:**

According to *Cambridge Dictionary*:

> **Emotional blackmail is the act of using a person's feelings of kindness, sympathy, or duty in order to persuade them to do something or feel something.**

When my mum used to tell me that boys blackmail girls, I used to wonder why. The going-out culture was already on the rise, and I didn't understand the point of force or blackmail. Thanks to all the serial killer series on Netflix, at least one thing is established: emotional blackmail is real and often happens because the person doing it has a sick mind. If you have seen the famous series "You," you know what I mean. A cute-looking guy can be all looney in his head for all you know.

How can you see the signs of looniness (if that's a word)?

Karen Doll, a consulting psychologist from Minnesota, mentioned in her article the characteristics of a blackmailer. I would say, these are rather the traits of a toxic person in your life. According to her, this blackmailer/toxic person can be a boyfriend, a fiancé, or anyone who knows you care about him.

The characteristics of a toxic person can be:

- Controlling what you do.

- Ignoring your concerns and pushback.
- Avoiding taking accountability.
- Constantly placing blame on others for their behaviours.
- Providing empty apologies.
- Using fear, obligation, threats, and guilt to get their way.
- Unwilling to compromise.
- Seemingly unconcerned about your needs.
- Rationalising their unreasonable behaviours and requests.
- Intimidate you until you do what they want.
- Blame you for something that you didn't do so that you feel you have to earn their affection.
- Accuse you of doing something you didn't do.
- Threaten to harm either you or themselves.

Why do you need to know this?

Because sooner or later, you will get into a relationship, and as much I wish you the best in your life, I want you to detect if something is not "right."

We live in very difficult and different times. Love is a beautiful emotion, but more often than not, it is exploited. You may say that this topic was not a topic to be discussed in a book of *hijab*. I say, this is exactly where it should be discussed. *Hijab* and coyness should be your strength and not a weakness in the hands of a perpetrator. I wish we never see a world where anything happens to a girl, *hijabi* or non-*hijabi*. But it is our job to prepare them nevertheless. As much as the world is opening up for women, these problems do persist, and in abundance. And we have to normalise talking about it. While mothers have to be vigilant, the girls have to take the necessary precautions too. A girl with her *hijab* should be strong enough to not take any nonsense rather than coiling in herself for fear of what people will say about this good little Muslim girl. If we don't provide a safe environment for the girls, it is on us. They should be made safe inside the house and outside.

Nevertheless, bad things happen, and we have to prepare ourselves to deal with them.

> **Love yourself enough to set boundaries. Your time and energy are precious. You get to choose how you use it. You teach people how to treat you by deciding what you will and won't accept.**
>
> — Anna Taylor

CONCLUSION

There Is No Tomorrow

Realise deeply that the present moment is all
you have. Make the NOW the primary focus of
your life.

— Eckhart Tolle

My dear girls, I have pretty much laid down all my cards; everything that I have collected over the years on this subject matter is in this book in black and white. The reasons, the whys, the hows, and everything that could go wrong. You should know everything about a business before getting into it; it's only fair.

With all said and done, are you in or not? I hope I have made it very clear that it's a no-judgement zone. If you were reading the book out of curiosity, that's good enough; if it was a light motivational read that kicks up your *imaan*, great; but if you were really thinking of taking up the *hijab*, what's stopping you?

You might be having the pre-*hijab* jitters. I completely get it. But you have to take the leap of faith sometime, right? What better time could it be than right after reading the book? You see, the purpose of the book was to give you the insight; from here on, you are all on your own. The more you delay it, the harder it becomes. If you are on the brink, take the fall; the wings will show up. If they don't, at least you could say that you tried.

There are a few things that might help you seal the deal, and I'll be as candid about them as ever. This is my last push and my last trial in getting you in. Just do it!

1. Faith:

I have said it many times. I have said it in many forms; *hijab* is the manifestation of your faith at the end of the day. You cannot start it, and you cannot go on with it, if it's not for the faith. Deepen that connection, girl. There is nothing but that at the end of the day. Get to know Allah; know what He does for you, the grand scheme of things—it is all there to facilitate you. You in person. Countless events have been in motion prior to you even making the *niyah* to get you to where you are today, learning about the rights and wrongs, and working up the courage. He has been there for you much before you even knew it. It's time that you get to know Him with His perfect names and His perfect attributes. Know that the purpose of *hijab* is to please only Him. Not your mom, dad, friends, or husband. Only Him. Say, *"La ilaha illa Allah,"* there is no God but Him, feel it run through your veins, and know He is even closer to you than your jugular vein, watching out for you even when you can't. Connect everything back to that statement. Know that you are doing it for the One who is the only God, and He wants to see you covered and protected and representing your faith. It is only from Him that you can draw strength.

2. Small steps:

Take a small step, but take it now. Start with a bandana, or casually cover your head like you forgot to take the covering off after the prayer. Do it slow but do it now. In Chapter 5, I have given a detailed brief on it. But this time, it's all about action. What one step will you take that will bring you closer to your ultimate goal? Decide and do it!

3. Dua, dua, and more dua!

If you want to but can't, make furious *duas*—like "everything is ending if you don't get it" kind of *dua*. Don't delay it. If *dua* is the one thing you'll do after reading the book, let that be your first step. And continue doing it until you actually get it.

The urgency of your *dua* defines how much you actually want it. If you still have lukewarm *duas*, go back to stage one, strengthen the connection but keep on making *duas*! Lukewarm is better than nothing. Don't lose sight of the goal, which is the ultimate pleasure of Allah. Do it! Do it now. Before you go on to my next point, pause and make *dua* for any weakness on this path.

4. Take away distractions:

Don't be distracted by *waswaas* now. This is the time when they will come with full force. "What if" is the diction of *shaitan*. It gives you doubts and takes you to the webs of scenarios that could happen. You could get hit by a car the moment you step on the road, but that doesn't stop you from getting out of the house, right? You need to be focussed right now. You might be having the thoughts like, "Let me be a better Muslim first" or "a more truthful person" or "a more helpful person" or "Let me fix my prayers first." Let me tell you, these open-ended goals will never let you start anything new. You can start wearing the *hijab* and work on all the above alongside. There is no this or that. It's all-inclusive, it's all a struggle—a struggle to be a better Muslim in entirety.

5. Visualise:

Your experience doesn't necessarily have to be a difficult one, or one which ends with a failure. You could succeed too; ever thought about that? You could really wear it and own it. How would you know if you don't try? Try visualising yourself entering a room full of people who praise you when you enter the room. Try visualising meeting Allah سُبْحَانَهُ وَتَعَالَىٰ and saying I tried my best for you! It could happen, you know. You need to take the leap to find out.

6. **Figure out the source of fear:**

You need to be honest and find out what really is that one thing which is stopping you. And take charge and stop that one thing. Fear of failure is more difficult to tackle than the failure itself. You need to know what is that one thing which if eliminated, you could easily wear the *hijab*. The external factors are there, and always will be, we can't do much about it. But we can certainly change the way we look at them. Brainstorm about how you can reduce the fear. Is it the fear of what people will say about the change? Start warming them about the idea, so that it's not too tough on them. If you fear you will look weird with the *hijab*; start trying new styles before you officially take it up. Face your fears. Only then the adrenaline will kick in.

7. **Don't be afraid to ask for help:**

You would be surprised how people come forward to help once you ask for it. But you have to ask for it. No one knows what you are struggling with. Talk to anyone who you think would understand—a friend, your mum, your mum's friend, or a teacher—and if no one else I am always here. It is my life's mission to help girls like you. I promise I will try my best to be there as much as I can, wherever you are on the globe. You know my name, my IG handle, and my website; just shoot away any question you like. Just don't be afraid to ask for help if you feel you need it.

That's all, folks. That's all I have for you in my tiny basket of advice. Now tell me one thing that you will do right after you close this book. You owe me one small action at least. What is that one tiny thing that will change in your life? I'll wait to hear from you. Remember I am always here for you, no matter which part of the world you are in. I really hope I was of some help. I really do. I really hope you take the leap wherever you are. I really hope you enjoy the ride while you are at it. And I really, really hope that Allah is pleased with you and you with Him.

Hijab starts with conviction and persists with perseverance. It has a huge impact on a person's overall performance as a Muslim. It serves as a constant reminder and a driving force for Muslim women to improve their relations with God and his people. Every time a girl fixes her *hijab* standing in front of a mirror, she is reminded of why is she doing it in the first place. For herself and her Lord. Let's get started.

> **The journey of a thousand miles begins with one step.**
>
> — Lao Tzu

GLOSSARY

Introduction:

Deen: الدين (Arabic/Urdu) Religion

Deeni: ديني (Urdu) One related to religion

Dunya: الدنيا (Arabic/Urdu) World/worldly

Jilbaab: جِلْبَاب (Arabic) Used in the Quran. Jilbaab is an outer garment/cloth that is worn on the head, draped around the body and totally covers a woman's form. It also refers to any long and loose-fitting coat

Chapter 1:

Abaya: عباية (Arabic/ Urdu) A full length outer garment/ coat worn by Muslim women; it's a variation of the Jilbaab.

Alhamdulillah: الحمد لله (Arabic) All thanks to Allah

Allah: الله God

Halwa: حلوى/حلوه (Arabic/Urdu) Arabic/Pakistani sweet

Hijab: حجاب (Arabic/Urdu) Head covering/scarf

Hijabi: حجابي (Urdu) A girl who covers her head

Mullah: الملا (Urdu) An educated Muslim trained in religious law and doctrine

Naqsh: نقش (Urdu) To imprint, to stamp

Shalwar Kameez: شلوار قميص (Urdu) Traditional dress of Pakistan comprising of a knee-length shirt and baggy pants

Wudu: (Arabic) وضوء (wuzu in Urdu) Ablution required before most acts of worship

سُبْحَانَهُ وَتَعَالَىٰ: (Arabic) (pronounced: Subhana-o-Ta'ala) Praised and exalted is He

Chapter 2:

Azaan: الأذان (Arabic/Urdu) Call for prayer

Burqa: البرقع (Urdu) Long, loose dress covering the whole body from head to feet, mostly worn with a veil. Another variation of Jilbaab.

Dupatta: دپٹہ (Urdu) Long scarf, part of Pakistani national dress

Fard: فرض (Arabic) (Farz in Urdu) Obligatory

Imaam: الإمام (Arabic/Urdu) The person who leads prayer in the mosque

InshaAllah: إن شاء الله (Arabic) If Allah wills

Molvi: مولوي (Urdu) An Islamic religious title given to Muslim religious scholars or teachers (Especially in South Asia)

Sahab: صاحب (Urdu) Mister

Walay: والي (Urdu) Possessor of something

Chapter 3:

Al Aleem: العليم (Arabic) The All-Knowing

Al Musawwir: المصور (Arabic) The Fashioner, One of the 99 names of Allah

Ameen: آمين (Arabic) Amen. May it be as it is

Ayah: آية (Arabic) (Ayat in Urdu) Verse

Dua: دعاء (Arabic/Urdu) Invocation

Gunah: گناہ (Urdu) Sin

Haram: حرام (Arabic/Urdu) Forbidden by Islamic law

Ibadah: عبادة (Arabic) (Ibadat in Urdu) Worship

Imaan/Iman: ايمان (Arabic/Urdu) Faith

Jannah: جنة (Arabic) (Jannat in Urdu) Paradise

Jahannum: جهنم (Arabic/Urdu) Hell

Niyyah: نِيَّةٌ (Arabic) (Niyyat in Urdu) Intention

Quran: القرآن Holy book of Muslims

Rabbul izzat: رب العزة (Arabic) The Lord of Dignity

Ramadan: رمضان (Arabic) (Ramzan in Urdu) One of the months in the Islamic calendar

Rehmah: الرحمة (Arabic) (Rehmat in Urdu) Mercy

Sawab: الثواب (Urdu) Reward

Taufeeq: التوفيق (Arabic/Urdu) Strength/Ability/help

Chapter 4

Aurah: عورة (Arabic) The intimate parts of the human body which must, according to Islam, be covered by clothing

Fitnah: فتنة (Arabic/Urdu) Temptation/trial/affliction

Hadith: حديث (Arabic/Urdu) Record of the traditions or sayings of Prophet Muhammad

Maghrib: المغرب (Arabic/Urdu) Sunset prayer

Mehram: محرم (Arabic/Urdu) Anyone who you are permanently forbidden to marry because of blood ties, marriage ties, and ties of having breastfed. A girl doesn't need to cover her hair in front of these family members e.g., brother, father, husband, and father-in-law

Non/Na–Mehram: نامحرم (Urdu) Anyone whom a girl needs to cover herself from. Includes strangers, cousins, and people outside the family

Rada: رضا (Arabic) If a child is suckled by someone other than the blood mother, it produces a legal impediment to marriage of foster-kinship, and refers to the fact that a wet nurse is considered related to the infant she nurses, and all the Islamic Laws applying to the real mother and her family applies to her and her family too

Sunnah: سُنَّة (Arabic) (Sunnat in Urdu) Refers to the traditions and practices of Prophet Muhammad that constitute a model for Muslims to follow

Chapter 5:

Kurtis: کرتیاں Plural of kurti; Indian blouse to be worn with jeans or pyjamas

Saris: ساڑھیاں Plural of sari, Indian traditional dress

Sharia: شریعہ Islamic law

Sheila: الشيلة (Arabic) Head scarf

Taqwa: تقوی (Arabic) Consciousness associated with God

waswaas: وسواس (Arabic) Satanic whispers

Chapter 6:

Al-Mudabbir: المدبر: (Arabic) The manager of all affairs

Ehsaan: إحسان (Arabic/Urdu) To do something perfectly

Nae'ma: نعمة (Arabic) (Na'emat in Urdu) Blessing

Tafseer: تفسير (Arabic) Refers to exegesis (critical explanation or interpretation of a text) of the Quran

Tajweed: تجويد (Arabic) The set of rules governing the way in which the words of the Quran should be pronounced during its recitation

ﷺ : (Arabic) Symbol for salle Allahu ailaihi wasallum i.e., Peace and blessings upon him

Chapter 7:

Azkaar: أذكار (plural of zikr) Remembrance of Allah

Huffadh: حفاظ/حافظ (Arabic) (Plural of Hafidh) (huffaz/ hafiz in Urdu) A person who has memorised the whole Quran

Ibadah: عبادة (Arabic) (ibadat in Urdu) Worship

Muhsineen: محسنين (Arabic) (Plural of Muhsin) One who does something perfectly

Ummah: أمة (Arabic) (Ummat in Urdu) Nation

جل جلاله : (Arabic) (Pronounced: Jalla jalalahu) May His Glory be glorified

رضي الله عنه : (Arabic) (Pronounced Radi Allahu anhu) May Allah be pleased with him

Chapter 8:

Eid Milan: عيد ملن (Urdu) Eid gathering/celebration

Rafeequl Aala: الرفيق الأعلى (Arabic) Most sublime intimate friend

Chapter 9:

Khushu: خشوع (Arabic) Humility

Masala: مصالحہ (Urdu) Indian spices

Paan masala: پان مصالحہ (Urdu) Pakistani mouth freshener

Salah: الصلاة (Arabic) prayer

Taraweeh: التراويح (Arabic) Long night prayers offered during the holy month of Ramadan

Chapter 10:

Akhirah: الآخرة (Arabic) Life after death

Istaghfar: الاستغفار (Arabic) Seeking forgiveness

Kafir: كافر (Arabic/urdu) Nonbeliever

mashaAllah: ما شاء الله (Arabic) What Allah has willed/expression of joy

Chapter 11:

صلاة استخارة : (Arabic) Special prayer of council with God

Conclusion:

La ilaha illa Allah: لا إله إلا الله (Arabic) There is no God but Allah

ABOUT THE AUTHOR

Kiran Shah is an internationally acclaimed artist, Emotional Intelligence, NLP and Corporate trainer and coach. She holds a Diploma in Islamic Education and has taught various religious and character-building courses. She writes for Hiba and The C Word Magazine and aims to help young Muslim girls become more confident and independent versions of themselves. She was recognised among "The Women at the Helm" by the Khaleej Times in 2018 for her artistic endeavours. In 2019, she displayed her work in Carrousal de Louvre, Paris and Moscow State Museum "Burganov House." Kiran lives in Dubai with her husband and four kids and loves to travel, read, and work out in her free time.

www.kiranshahofficial.com

www.instagram.com/pink_shoes_and_jilbaab

kiranshah@hotmail.com

www.ingramcontent.com/pod-product-compliance
Lightning Source LLC
Chambersburg PA
CBHW021439080526
44588CB00009B/601